Pressure Cooker & Air Fryer All-in-one Cookbook

Easy & Mouthwatering Recipes for Quick & Tasty Everyday Meals

Blake Griffiths

ISBN: 978-1797626581

Contents

BEEF 77

DESSERTS 120

Introduction

Welcome to the Pressure Cooker and Air Fryer All-in-one Cookbook!

This brand new cooking appliance has it all! The new Pressure Cooker and Air Fryer Multicooker is a combination of pressure cooker and air fryer that lets you cook delicious and healthy meals in no time. You're also going to love my cookbook! I've come up with amazing and tasty recipes to share with you. I'm sure everyone in your family will enjoy them.

In this cookbook, the recipes are all easy and quick to make. They each come with a full ingredient list and detailed instructions. No matter how inexperienced you think you are in the kitchen, or with the machine, you will have no problem at all making these wonderful recipes!

The Multicooker is a combination pressure cooker and air fryer. It's easy to use, saves you loads of time, and clean up is a breeze.

Not only does my cookbook have amazing recipes for you, but I will also show you how you can make the most of the Multicooker using all of its different settings and controls. If you have one cookbook in your kitchen, this is the one. Whether you're a seasoned cook or a novice, my cookbook will help you get super tasty, healthy meals on the table in no time at all.

The Multicooker is where you get the best of an instant pot with an air fryer, so you can take foods from tender pressure cooked to a crispy finish in as little as 30 minutes. Crispy chicken, soups and stews, casseroles. Appetizer, entrees, and desserts... I have a recipe for you!

WHAT IS THE PRESSURE COOKER & AIR FRYER ALL-IN-ONE?

It's the most versatile, easy to use kitchen appliance you will ever own. It's a slow cooker, electric pressure cooker, air fryer, sauté pan, and rice cooker all in one.

This combination of pressure cooker and air fryer will cook your food faster and more efficiently than any other tool in your kitchen. You can make all of your favorite meals – the classic roast and chicken soup, chili and stews – and then you can use my recipes to make dishes in the Multicooker that you didn't think were possible. Like breakfast dishes and desserts.

Don't let all the functions and settings on the Multicooker intimidate you! Each of my recipes gives you exact instructions on what functions to use and what buttons to press.

BENEFITS!

Using the Multicooker as a pressure cooker, you can make juicy and tender meals in no time, full of flavor and delicious taste. Then using the crisping lid, the Multicooker becomes the ideal air fryer, letting you enjoy crispy fried foods without using oil. You'll love how you can use multiple functions together, such as pressure cooking and then air frying. Or you can use one single function, such as the slow cook setting. The possibilities are endless!

One pot cooking

Using just one pot you can turn boring soup and casserole dishes into delicious meals of wonder. No more pulling out multiple pots to make dinner at the end of a long day. Just get all the ingredients together, put them into the Multicooker, set the pot…and it does all the work for you. All in one pot!

Frees up kitchen space

No matter what size your kitchen is, it seems you never enough room on the counter or in your cupboards for all those kitchen appliances that are supposed to make your life easier. Now you can get rid of those other appliances and free up valuable space. The New Multicooker does everything all those other appliances did – all in one.

Cook frozen foods

How many times have you forgotten to take the chicken out of the freezer so it's ready to cook when you get home? If you're like me, too many times to count. Those days are gone! The New Multicooker takes frozen foods, quickly de-thaws them, and then cooks them to perfection. All at the same time.

Cook nutritious meals

The New Multicooker lets you cook nutritious meals by retaining all those healthy nutrients. The pressure cooking and slow cooking functions cook foods fast and efficiently, so they're tender and juicy.

Cook meals in one

You can cook complete meals in the Multicooker. It does it all, cooking roast chicken, potatoes, and your side of steamed vegetables so that everything is ready when you are!

The incredible convenience of leftovers!

You can cook as much or as little as you want. Make just enough for one family meal. Or make extra so you can enjoy leftovers the next day. Or take some for lunch!

Clean up is done in no time

No one wants to spend time after dinner scrubbing pots and pans. Clean up is done in no time with the Multicooker. The ceramic-coated pot is non-stick, so all it takes is a quick wash in soapy water – and you're out of the kitchen and on to better things!

HOW TO USE THE BUTTONS

Using the New Multicooker is straightforward and easy…you'll have no problem getting to know the functions and settings.

Pressure

The setting that you'll probably use most often is the pressure-cooking setting. Many of my recipes use this function. For each of my recipes, you just need to select the pressure and the time needed – it's almost like using your oven. Foods are cooked at a high temperature under pressure. When the cooking time is complete, pressure is released from the Pressure Cooker…and it's time to eat!

Steam

One of the healthiest reasons to use the Multicooker is for the steam function. Water is boiled in the Pressure Cooker and the resulting steam flows up into the steaming rack which sits in the inner chamber of the pot. Vegetables and other foods are gently steamed, retaining not only their nutrients, but they stay nice and crispy as well! No more soggy vegetables that no one wants to eat.

The steam function is also ideal for cooking fish and seafood, which is more delicate to cook than meats and chicken. The steaming process seals in flavor and moisture. As with vegetables, use the steaming rack so the fish isn't sitting on the bottom of the pot. Follow directions in my recipes for cooking time so you don't overcook fish.

Slow cooker

Some foods taste richer when cooked slowly over a few hours. Use the slow cooker function when you want foods to cook longer to bring out the intense taste of spices and herbs in soups, stews, and casseroles. Prepare the recipe ingredients in the morning, or the night before, and toss into the Multicooker. Cook at high or low, depending on how long you want the dish to simmer. And let the cooker do its thing. Nothing's better than coming home at the end of the day to a delicious home cooked meal!

Sear/Sauté

Many of my recipes use the browning and sautéing function. The Multicooker comes with five stove top temperature settings so you can get the same results in the cooker as you would using a frying pan – just add a bit of oil. You can use the brown/sauté function to simmer foods, gently cook them, or sear them at high temperatures. This is a great way to sear meats to seal in juicy flavors before fully cooking in the Multicooker. The sautéing setting is also perfect for cooking vegetables – just sauté and serve them over a bed of cooked rice.

Air Crisp

Use the New Multicooker as an air fryer and you'll never go back to making roast chicken in the oven. The air crisp function lets you bake, broil, and roast foods to perfection. They'll come out golden and crisp, caramelized to excellence. The Multicooker comes with a basket so you can cook and crisp using the air fryer function. All without the use of any oil, unless called for in my recipes. You can even cook frozen prepacked onion rings in just a few minutes. No more getting out the fryer and pouring in the oil!

Pressure cook foods to seal in the juices and then use the crisping lid to get a nice crispy finish. This is a super way to cook an entire roast chicken or roast. All of the moisture and taste is cooked into the chicken, with the crisping giving the chicken a lovely roasted flavor sensation.

Bake/Roast/Broil

You'll love the convenience of the Multicooker when it works like a convection oven. You'll be able to bake amazing casseroles, roast the perfect pork loin, and broil the top of dishes so the cheese is melted and golden. All with the bake/roast/broil functions.

Dehydrate

Some models of the Multicooker have the dehydrating function. This is the ideal way to make snacks for you and your family to enjoy any time, such as banana chips, dried apple slices, and beef jerky.

Please note that cooking times may vary depending on the cooking quantities or the exact cooking appliance model you are using.

QUICK COOKING GUIDE FOR BEST RESULTS

The New Multicooker is simple to use! And each of my recipes gives you exact directions so you don't need to guess what buttons to push. Here are some quick tips to get you started.

Choose the recipe

Choose one of the recipes from my cookbook. Maybe you're looking for a quick meal that cooks in 30 minutes. Or perhaps you have time for the cooker to function as a slow cooker while you're gone for the day. No matter what you're in the mood for, I have a recipe for you.

Prep the Multicooker

Read through to the end of the recipe so you know what function you're going to be using – then get the Multicooker ready to go with one of the following.

Prepare your ingredients

Follow my recipe and prep all the ingredients that go into the dish. Add them directly to the Multicooker or to one of the cooking accessories that you're using for the recipe.

Set the function, temperature, and time

Select the function and temperature according to the recipe directions. Then set the required time. Follow instructions exactly. When you've made your favorite recipes more than once, you'll know if you need to adjust the temperature or time.

Toss or turn food if needed

Some of my recipes require that you turn the food during the cooking process to prevent sticking and so the food gets even crispiness when cooking.

Serve and enjoy!

When the timer goes off your meal is ready to go! After using, let the Multicooker cool completely before taking apart and cleaning. Soak any of the cooking accessories in hot, soapy water if needed. Never use abrasive cleaners to clean the cooker.

THE RECIPES

Once you make just one of the recipes in my cookbook, you'll be hooked on using this all in one appliance for all your meals! My cookbook has all my favorite recipes, ones that I cook over and over again for my family and friends.

Whether you're looking for fast and quick healthy recipes for a weeknight meal, or want a more decadent dish to impress guests, I have just the recipe you need.

To get you started using the New Multicooker, I've put together these recipes that include everything from appetizers to side dishes and main meals to desserts. I've included a wide range of cuisines so there's something for every taste. You'll find recipes using meat, poultry, and seafood. Don't forget the vegetables, so on those days when you want a vegetarian meal, you can easily find a tasty recipe.

All my recipes have a full ingredient list and instructions that are easy to follow. Some recipes only require a few ingredients while others are a bit more complicated – but definitely worth it! You'll quickly find out just how versatile and amazing the Multicooker is. And wonder how you ever cooked without it.

Now that you know all about what the cooker can do, it's time to start cooking and discover the beautiful recipes in my cookbook!

CONVERSIONS CHART

Unit:	Equals:	Also Equals:
1 teaspoon	⅓ tablespoon	¼ fluid ounce
1 tablespoon	3 teaspoons	½ fluid ounce
⅛ cup	2 tablespoons	1 fluid ounce
¼ cup	4 tablespoons	2 fluid ounces
1/3 cup	¼ cup plus 4 teaspoons	2 ¾ fluid ounces
½ cup	8 tablespoons	4 fluid ounces
1 cup	½ pint	8 fluid ounces
1 pint	2 cups	16 fluid ounces
1 quart	4 cups	32 fluid ounces
1 liter	1 quart plus ¼ cup	4 ¼ cups
1 gallon	4 quarts	16 cups

SNACKS & APPETIZERS

FINGER-LICKING BARBECUE CHICKEN WINGS

Football season, movie night, or lazy day, these barbecued wings will satisfy your cravings. They are spicy with that kick to run your adrenaline high so make sure to use a cheesy to help tame the spiciness.

Preparation Time: 5 minutes | Cooking Time: 25 minutes | Servings: 6

Ingredients:

3 lb Chicken Wingettes

3 tbsp Cajun Garlic Powder

Salt to taste

¼ cup Barbecue Sauce

½ cup Hot Sauce

¼ cup Butter, melted

½ cup Water

Directions:

1. Pat the wingettes dry with a paper towel and put them in a bowl. Season them with Cajun garlic powder and salt.

2. Open the cooker, pour in the water, and fit in the reversible rack. Arrange the wingettes on top, close the lid, secure the pressure valve, and select Pressure mode for 5 minutes. Press Start/Stop to start cooking.

3. Once the timer has ended, do a natural pressure release for 10 minutes, and then a quick pressure release to let out any more steam. Open the lid.

4. Remove the wings with tongs to a crisp basket and add the butter, half of the hot sauce and half of the barbecue sauce. Stir the chicken until well coated in the sauce.

5. Insert the basket in the pot and close the crisping lid. Select Air Crisp, set to 380 degrees F, and cook for 10 minutes. Select Start/Stop.

6. Once nice and crispy, remove them to a bowl, and top with the remaining barbecue and hot sauces. Stir and serve the chicken with a cheese dip.

Nutrition facts Nutrition facts per serving:

Calories 361; Fat 13.7g; Sodium 178mg; Carbs 9g; Protein 35.7g

PARMESAN CROQUETTES

Just like croquettes, I enjoy this creamy, cheesy rice arancini because they are such a yummy delight. Consider them one of the first in your appetizer menu because your guests will love them. Make sure to make plenty too because they finish fast.

Preparation Time: 15 minutes | Cooking Time: 27 minutes | Servings: 6

Ingredients

½ cup olive oil, plus 1 tablespoon

1 onion, diced

2 garlic cloves, minced

5 cups chicken stock

½ cup apple vinegar

2 cups rice

1½ cups grated Parmesan cheese

1 cup chopped green beans

1 tsp salt

1tsp freshly ground black pepper

2 cups fresh panko breadcrumbs

2 eggs

Directions

1. Choose Sear/Sauté on the pot and add in 1 tablespoon of oil and onion. Sauté the onion until translucent, add the garlic and cook further for 2 minutes or until the garlic starts getting fragrant. Stir in the stock, vinegar, and rice. Seal the pressure lid, choose Pressure, set to High, and set the time to 7 minutes. Press Start/Stop.
2. After cooking, perform a natural pressure release for 10 minutes.
3. Stir in the Parmesan cheese, green beans, salt, and pepper to mash the rice until a risotto forms. Spoon the mixture into a bowl and set aside to cool completely.
4. Clean the pot and in a bowl, combine the breadcrumbs and the remaining olive oil. In another bowl, lightly beat the eggs.
5. Form 12 croquettes out of the rice mixture or as many as you can get. Dip each into the beaten eggs, and coat in the breadcrumb mixture.
6. Put the rice balls in the Cook & Crisp basket in a single layer.
7. Close the crisping lid, choose Air Crisp, set the temperature to 390 degrees F, and set the time to 12 minutes. Choose Start/Stop to begin frying or until the balls are crisp and golden brown. At the 6-minute mark, turn the croquettes.
8. Allow coolling before serving. Serve with tangy relish.

Nutrition facts Nutrition facts per serving:

Calories 769; Fat 32g; Sodium 1348mg; Carbs 91g; Protein 27g

CHEESY GREEN BITES

These greenly bites are a representation of everything that kale and artichoke can be used for. Both greens easily combine with cheese, cream, and many Ingredients, so for making these, I live you to swap or add some Ingredients to make it a personal affair.

Preparation Time: 15 minutes | Cooking Time: 15 minutes | Servings: 8

Ingredients

¼ cup chopped kale

¼ cup chopped artichoke hearts

¼ cup ricotta cheese

2 tbsp grated Parmesan cheese

¼ cup goat cheese

1 large egg white

1 tsp dried basil

1 lemon, zested

½ tsp salt

½ tsp freshly ground black pepper

4 sheets frozen phyllo dough, thawed

1 tbsp olive oil

Directions

1. In a bowl, mix the kale, artichoke hearts, ricotta cheese, parmesan cheese, goat cheese, egg white, basil, lemon zest, salt, and pepper.

2. Close the crisping lid, choose Air Crisp, set the temperature to 370 degrees F, and the time to 5 minutes. Press Start/Stop.

3. Then, place a phyllo sheet on a clean flat surface. Brush with olive oil, place a second phyllo sheet on the first, and brush with oil. Continue layering to form a pile of four oiled sheets.

4. Working from the short side, cut the phyllo sheets into 8 strips. Cut the strips in half to form 16 strips.

5. Spoon 1 tablespoon of filling onto one short side of every strip. Fold a corner to cover the filling to make a triangle; continue folding repeatedly to the end of the strip, creating a triangle-shaped phyllo packet. Repeat the process with the other phyllo bites.

6. Open the Ccisping lid and place the bites in the basket in one layer. Close the lid, choose Air Crisp, set the temperature to 350 degrees F, and the timer to 10 minutes. Press Start/Stop to begin baking.

7. At the 5-minute mark, open the lid, and flip the bites. Return the basket to the pot and close the lid to continue baking. Once the timer beeps, check to ensure the bites are cooked all the way through.

Nutrition facts Nutrition facts per serving:

Calories 75; Fat 4g; Sodium 310mg; Carbs 7g; Protein 3g

TASTY CHICKEN BALLS

With the games here always, these balls should not depart from your home. They sit in the buffalo sauce and chicken flavors like we love in buffalo wings and are just perfect. Or simply, make them into a complete meal over a bed of noodles.

Preparation Time: 10 minutes | Cooking Time: 25 minutes | Servings: 6

Ingredients

1 pound ground chicken

1 green bell pepper, minced

2 celery stalks, minced

¼ cup crumbled queso fresco

¼ cup hot sauce

¼ cup panko breadcrumbs

1 egg

2 tablespoons melted butter

½ cup water

Directions

1. In a bowl, combine the chicken, bell pepper, celery, queso fresco, hot sauce, breadcrumbs, and egg. Form balls (approximately the size of golf balls) out of the mixture.
2. Choose Sear/Sauté on the pot and set to High. Pour in the melted butter and fry the meatballs in batches until lightly browned on all sides. Use a slotted spoon to remove the meatballs onto a plate.
3. Put the Cook & Crisp basket in the pot. Pour in the water and put all the meatballs in the basket.
4. Seal the pressure lid, choose Pressure, set to High, and set the timer to 5 minutes. Hit Start/Stop.
5. When done cooking, perform a quick pressure release and carefully open the lid.
6. Close the crisping lid, press Air Crisp button set the temperature to 360 degrees F and set the time to 10 minutes. Choose Start/Stop.
7. At the 5-minute mark, shake the meatballs. Cook until the chicken balls are crispy to your desire.

Nutrition facts Nutrition facts per serving:

Calories 204; Fat 13g; Sodium 566mg; Carbs 5g; Protein 16g

BUFFALO CHICKEN BALLS WITH ROQUEFORT SAUCE

Buffalo goes with everything either as an appetizer or a sauce for the main meal. In 20 minutes, this dish should be ready to bite into. Enjoy with gladness!

Preparation Time: 10 minutes | Cooking Time: 24 minutes | Servings: 4

Ingredients:

1 lb Ground Chicken

2 tbsp Buffalo wing sauce

1 Egg, beaten

Salt and Pepper, to taste

2 tbsp Minced Garlic

2 tbsp Olive Oil

5 tbsp Hot Sauce

2 tbsp chopped Green Onions + extra for garnish

For the sauce:

½ cup Roquefort Cheese, crumbled

¼ tbsp Heavy Cream

2 tbsp Mayonnaise

Juice from ½ Lemon

2 tbsp Olive Oil

Directions:

1. Mix all salsa ingredients in a bowl until uniform and creamy, and refrigerate.
2. Add the ground chicken, salt, garlic, and two tablespoons of green onions. Mix well with your hands.
3. Rub your hands with some oil and form bite-size balls out of the mixture.
4. Lay onto your crisp basket fryer basket. Spray with cooking spray.
5. Select Air Crisp, set the temperature to 385 degrees F and the time to 14
6. minutes. At the 7-minute mark, turn the meatballs.
7. Meanwhile, add the hot sauce and butter to a bowl and microwave them until the butter melts. Mix the sauce with a spoon.
8. Pour the hot sauce mixture and a half cup of water over the meatballs.
9. Close the lid, secure the pressure valve, and select Sear/Sauté mode on High Pressure for 10 minutes. Press Start/Stop.
10. Once the timer has ended, do a quick pressure release. Dish the meatballs.
11. Garnish with green onions, and serve with Roquefort sauce.

Nutrition facts Nutrition facts per serving:

Calories 424; Fat 38g; Sodium 204mg; Carbs 7g; Protein 26g

PROSCIUTTO WRAPPED ASPARAGUS WITH BEEN DIP

The Asparagus can be steamed and served not only as a side dish, but they can also be fused up to be snacked on. I love this easy fusion that gets ready in no time. Got a big task to finish? Make these wrapped asparagus and munch on them as you work. Trust me, and you will not feel the heat of the workload.

Preparation Time: 5 minutes | Cooking Time: 10 minutes | Servings: 6

Ingredients:

1 lb Asparagus, stalks trimmed

10 oz Prosciutto, thinly sliced

Cooking Spray

For the Dip:

1 cup canned white beans

1 medium onion, diced

2 cloves of garlic, minced

2 medium jalapeños, chopped

1 cup crushed Tomatoes

1 cup vegetable broth

1 ½ tbsp olive oil

1 tsp. paprika

¾ tsp. sea salt

½ tsp. chili powder

Directions:

1. Open the cooker and add the white beans, onion, jalapeños, garlic, tomatoes, broth, oil, paprika, chili powder, and salt.
2. Close the lid, secure the pressure valve, and select Pressure mode on High for 8 minutes. Press Start/Stop.
3. Once the timer has ended, do a quick pressure release, and open the pot.
4. Transfer the ingredients to a food processor, and blend until creamy and smooth. Set aside. Wrap each asparagus with a slice of prosciutto from top to bottom.
5. Grease the crisp basket with cooking spray, and add in the wrapped asparagus. Close the crisping lid, select Air Crisp mode at 370 degrees F and set the time to 8 minutes. Press Start/Stop. At the 4-minute mark, turn the bombs.
6. Remove the wrapped asparagus onto a plate and serve with bean dip.

Nutrition facts Nutrition facts per serving:

Calories 154; Fat 12.4g; Sodium 240mg; Carbs 3g; Protein 9.4g

BEEF AND CABBAGE DUMPLINGS

Crispy dumplings never got better, thanks to the Multicooker because they don't turn soggy and the beef filling just sits soft and juicy in the crunchy wrap. Now, there's no way my oven is making me dumplings anymore. I look forward to serving these at my next party.

Preparation Time: 20 minutes | Cooking Time: 12 minutes | Servings: 8

Ingredients

8 ounces ground beef

½ cup grated cabbage

1 carrot, grated

1 large egg, beaten

1 garlic clove, minced

2 tbsp coconut aminos

½ tbsp melted ghee

½ tbsp ginger powder

½ tsp salt

½ tsp freshly ground black pepper

20 wonton wrappers

2 tbsp olive oil

Directions

1. Close crisping lid. Preheat your cooker by choosing Air Crisp at 390 degrees F for 5 minutes.
2. In a large bowl, mix the beef, cabbage, carrot, egg, garlic, coconut aminos, ghee, ginger, salt, and black pepper.
3. Put the wonton wrappers on a clean flat surface and spoon 1 tablespoon of the beef mixture into the middle of each wrapper. Run the edges of the wrapper with a little water; fold the wrapper to cover the filling into a semi-circle shape and pinch the edges to seal. Then, brush the dumplings with olive oil.
4. Lay the dumplings in the preheated basket, choose Air Crisp, set the temperature to 390 degrees F, and set the time to 12 minutes. Choose Start/Stop.
5. At the 6-minute mark, open the lid, pull out the basket and shake the dumplings. Return the basket to the pot and close the lid to continue frying until the dumplings are crispy to your desire.

Nutrition facts Nutrition facts per serving:

Calories 186; Fat 11g; Sodium 424mg; Carbs 13g; Protein 8g

EASY CRISPY WINGS

I couldn't have left out hot chicken wings for the fact that it is a go-to appetizer and because they cook quick and crispy with the Multicooker. What's next, just grab your frozen wings and let's get some heat rolling in.

Preparation Time: 10 minutes | Cooking Time: 20 minutes | Servings: 4

Ingredients

½ cup water

½ cup sriracha sauce

2 tbsp butter, melted

1 tbsp lemon juice

8 chicken wings

½ tsp hot paprika

Cooking spray

Directions

1. Mix the water, sriracha, butter and lemon juice in the pot. In the Cook & Crisp basket, put the wings, and then the basket into the pot. Seal the pressure lid.

2. Choose Pressure, set to High, set the timer at 5 minutes, and choose Start/Stop.

3. When the timer is done reading, perform a quick pressure release, and carefully open the lid.

4. Pour the paprika all over the chicken and oil with cooking spray.

5. Cover the crisping lid. Choose Air Crisp, set the temperature to 375 degrees F, and the timer to 15 minutes. Choose Start to commence frying.

6. After half the cooking time, open the crisping lid, shake the wings. Oil the chicken again with cooking spray and return the basket to the pot.

7. Close the lid and continue cooking until the wingettes are crispy.

Nutrition facts Nutrition facts per serving:

Calories 405; Fat 30g; Sodium 1782mg; Carbs 4g; Protein 28g

BACON & CHEESE LOADED SWEET POTATOES

I drool when my potatoes are golden brown and oozing with flavor. Then, is the time to top them with everything I like; bacon, cream, cheese, jalapenos, just about anything that I am in the mood for. So, why not join the club? Top and enjoy!

Preparation Time: 10 minutes | Cooking Time: 30 minutes | Servings: 4

Ingredients

12 ounces sweet potatoes

1 teaspoon melted butter

¼ cup shredded Monterey Jack cheese

¼ cup buttermilk

2 slices bacon, cooked and crumbled

1 tablespoon chopped scallions

Salt to taste

Directions

1. Close crisping lid. Preheat your cooker by choosing Air Crisp at 390 degrees F for 5 minutes.
2. Toss the sweet potatoes with the melted butter until evenly coated.
3. Add to the Cook & Crisp basket. Close the lid, choose Air Crisp, set the temperature to 345 degrees F, and set the time to 30 minutes. Press Start/Stop.
4. After 15 minutes, open the lid, pull out the basket and shake the potatoes.
5. At the 15-minute mark, check the potatoes to see if they're crisped to your liking. In a bowl, mix cheese, buttermilk, bacon, and scallions, season with salt and set aside.
6. Take out the potatoes from the basket and halve the potatoes lengthways. Top with the bacon-cheese filling and serve.

Nutrition facts Nutrition facts per serving:

Calories 154; Fat 8g; Sodium 152mg; Carbs 16g; Protein 5g

TRADITIONAL PAO DE QUEIJO

Just a big snack that you want to have by you just in case some hunger pangs pop in unexpectedly. You can also make them as appetizers to warm your guests up for a heavier meal being prepared.

Preparation Time: 15 minutes | Cooking Time: 20 minutes | Servings: 4

Ingredients:

2 cups All-purpose flour

1 cup Milk

A pinch of salt

2 Eggs, cracked into a bowl

2 cups grated Parmesan Cheese

½ cup Olive Oil

Directions:

1. Grease the crisp basket with cooking spray and set aside.
2. Put the cooker on Medium and select Sear/Sauté mode.
3. Add the milk, oil, and salt, and let boil. Add the flour and mix it vigorously with a spoon.
4. Let the mixture cool. Once cooled, use a hand mixer to mix the dough well, and add the eggs and cheese while still mixing. The dough should be thick and sticky.
5. Use your hands to make 14 balls out of the mixture, and put them in the greased basket. Put the basket in the pot and close the crisping lid.
6. Select Air Crisp, set the temperature to 380 degrees F and set the timer to 15 minutes.
7. At the 7-minute mark, shake the balls.
8. Serve with lemon aioli, garlic mayo or ketchup.

Nutrition facts Nutrition facts per serving:

Calories 625; Fat 34g; Sodium 304mg; Carbs 54g; Protein 26g

BREAKFAST & BRUNCH

RICH GRITS WITH GRUYERE CHEESE AND BACON

A milky cheesy grits dish has always been my favorite heavy breakfast option. They are tasty and satisfying; I skip brunch and snacks when I take them. Making them with my new cookerPot makes life easier and faster, and I bet it will work for you too.

Preparation Time: 10 minutes | Cooking Time: 10 minutes | Servings: 4

Ingredients:

3 slices smoked Bacon, diced
1 ½ cups grated Gruyere Cheese
1 cup ground Grits
2 tsp Butter

Salt and Black Pepper
½ cup Water
½ cup Milk

Directions:

1. To preheat the cooker, select Sear/Sauté mode and set to HIGH pressure. Cook bacon until crispy, about 5 minutes. Set aside.
2. Add the grits, butter, milk, water, salt, and pepper to the pot and stir using a spoon. Close the pressure lid and secure the pressure valve.
3. Choose the Pressure mode and cook for 3 minutes on High. Press Start/Stop.
4. Once the timer has ended, turn the vent handle and do a quick pressure release. Add in cheddar cheese and give the pudding a good stir with the same spoon.
5. Close crisping lid, press BAKE/ROAST button and cook for 8 minutes on 370 degrees F. Press Start key.
6. When ready, dish the cheesy grits into serving bowls and spoon over the crisped bacon.
7. Serve right away with toasted bread.

Nutrition facts Nutrition facts per serving:

Calories 280; Fat 20.6g; Sodium 325mg; Carbs 8g; Protein 13.8g

RICOTTA & STRAWBERRY-FILLED FRENCH TOAST

French toast has always been a thing for me since childhood. I have learned to make them with variety by mix matching Ingredients over the years. Here, is my strawberry version giving the toasts some added taste, color, and fruity aroma?

Preparation Time: 15 minutes | Cooking Time: 25 minutes | Servings: 5

Ingredients

4 eggs

¼ cup milk

1 tbsp sugar mixed with 1 tsp cinnamon powder

Cooking spray

6 slices brioche, cubed

3 strawberries, sliced, divided

2 tbsp brown sugar, divided

¼ cup ricotta cheese, at room temperature

½ cup water

2 tablespoons butter, sliced

¼ cup chopped almonds

2 tablespoons honey

Directions

1. In a medium mixing bowl, combine the eggs, milk, and cinnamon sugar, Set aside.
2. Grease a baking dish with cooking spray and arrange half the brioche cubes in the dish in a single layer. Layer half the strawberry slices over the bread and dust with 1 tablespoon of brown sugar.
3. Spread the ricotta cheese on top of the bread and strawberries. Make another layer of bread, ricotta cheese, strawberries, and brown sugar.
4. Pour the egg mixture over the bread layers ensuring to coat the bread completely.
5. Pour the water into the pot. Fix the pan on the reversible rack, then put the rack with the pan in the pot. Seal the pressure lid position, choose Pressure and set to High. Set timer to 20 minutes. Choose Start/Stop to toast.
6. When done cooking, perform a quick pressure release to let out all the pressure, and carefully open the lid.
7. Top the French toast with the sliced butter, almonds, and honey.
8. Close the crisping lid. Hit Bake/Roast button, and cook for 5 minutes at 390 degrees F.
9. Serve immediately with yogurt and more strawberries.

Nutrition facts Nutrition facts per serving:

Calories 448; Fat 16g; Sodium 461mg; Carbs 66g; Protein 13g

CRISPY SCOTCH EGGS IN SAUSAGE

Scotch eggs are a hearty breakfast, lunch or appetizer option depending on what mood you are in. Instead of the boring regular, these are wrapped with sausage and then crisped. Eggs cook soft with the pressure cooker, so it is a cheerful bite in.

Preparation Time: 10 minutes | Cooking Time: 18 minutes | Servings: 4

Ingredients

1 cup water

4 eggs

Cooking spray

12 ounces Italian sausage patties

1 cup panko breadcrumbs

2 tablespoons melted unsalted butter

Directions

1. Pour 1 cup of water into the inner pot. Put in the reversible rack place the eggs on the rack. Seal the pressure lid, choose Pressure, set to High, and the cook time to 3 minutes. Press Start/Stop.

2. After cooking, perform a quick pressure release, and carefully open the lid.

3. Use tongs to pick up the eggs into an ice bath. Allow cooling for 3 to 4 minutes or until cool enough to handle. Peel the eggs to keep the egg whites intact and blot dry with a clean napkin.

4. Pour the water out of the inner pot and return the pot to the base. Grease the reversible rack with cooking spray and place in the pot.

5. Preheat your cooker by closing the crisping id; choose Air Crisp, set the temperature to 360 degrees F and the timer to 4 minutes. Press Start/Stop.

6. Meanwhile, place an egg on each sausage patty. Carefully pull the sausage around the egg and seal the edges.

7. In a small bowl, mix the breadcrumbs with the melted butter. One at a time, dredge the sausage-covered eggs in the crumbs while pressing into the breadcrumbs for a thorough coat.

8. Open the crisping lid and place the eggs on the rack. Close the crisping lid; choose Air Crisp, adjust the temperature to 360 degrees F, and the cook time to 15 minutes. Press Start/Stop to start crisping.

9. When the timer has ended, carefully remove the eggs and allow cooling for several minutes. Slice the eggs in half and serve.

Nutrition facts Nutrition facts per serving:

Calories 460; Fat 33g; Sodium 642mg; Carbs 18g; Protein 22g

SALMON VEGGIE CAKES

How about you leave salmon off the dinner list tomorrow and have it late in the morning? Sounds like a great idea, right? These cakes are made with veggies and some aromatic spices to set your mood up for the rest of the day's work.

Preparation Time: 10 minutes | Cooking Time: 30 minutes | Servings: 4

Ingredients:

2 (5 oz) packs Steamed Salmon Flakes

1 Red Onion, chopped

Salt and Black Pepper to taste

1 tsp Garlic Powder

2 tbsp Olive Oil

1 Red Bell Pepper, seeded and chopped

4 tbsp Butter, divided

3 Eggs, cracked into a bowl

1 cup Breadcrumbs

4 tbsp Mayonnaise

2 tsp Worcestershire Sauce

¼ cup chopped Parsley

Directions:

1. Turn on the cooker and select Sear/Sauté mode on High pressure.
2. Heat the oil and add half of the butter. Once it has melted, add the onions and the chopped red bell peppers. Cook for 6 minutes while stirring occasionally. Press Start/Stop.
3. In a mixing bowl, add salmon flakes, sautéed red bell pepper and onion, breadcrumbs, eggs, mayonnaise, Worcestershire sauce, garlic powder, salt, pepper, and parsley.
4. Use a spoon to mix well while breaking the salmon into the tiny pieces. Use your hands to mold 4 patties out of the mixture.
5. Add the remaining butter to melt, and when melted, add the patties. Fry for 4 minutes, flipping once.
6. Then, close the crisping lid, select Bake/Roast mode and bake for 4 minutes on 320 degrees F. Remove them onto a wire rack to rest.
7. Serve the cakes with a side of lettuce and potato salad with a mild drizzle of herb vinaigrette.

Nutrition facts Nutrition facts per serving:

Calories 373; Fat 25.5g; Sodium 440mg; Carbs 11.2g; Protein 21.4g

EGG, SAUSAGE CHORIZO & CHEESE CAKE

I can't get enough excitement out of this "sweet" mix. Rather than having regular boiled eggs, or scrambled eggs, make this casserole loaded with protein, sweet peppers, and some early morning spice.

Preparation Time: 15 minutes | Cooking Time: 10 minutes | Servings: 6

Ingredients:

8 Eggs, cracked into a bowl

8 oz Chorizo Sausage, chopped

3 Bacon Slices, chopped

1 large Green Bell Pepper, chopped

1 large Red Bell Pepper, chopped

1 cup chopped Green Onion

1 cup grated Cheddar Cheese

1 tsp Red Chili Flakes

Salt and Black Pepper to taste

½ cup Milk

4 slices Bread, cut into ½-inch cubes

2 cups Water

Directions:

1. Add the eggs, sausage chorizo, bacon slices, green and red bell peppers, green onion, chili flakes, cheddar cheese, salt, pepper, and milk to a bowl and use a whisk to beat them together.

2. Grease a bundt pan with cooking spray and pour the egg mixture into it. After, drop the bread slices in the egg mixture all around while using a spoon to push them into the mixture.

3. Open the cooker, pour in water, and fit the rack at the center of the pot. Place bundt pan on the rack and seal the pressure lid.

4. Select Pressure mode on High pressure for 6 minutes, and press Start/Stop.

5. Once the timer goes off, press Start/Stop, do a quick pressure release. Run a knife around the egg in the bundt pan, close the crisping lid and cook for another 4 minutes on Bake/Roast on 380 degrees F.

6. When ready, place a serving plate on the bundt pan, and then, turn the egg bundt over. Use a knife to cut the egg into slices. Serve with a sauce of your choice.

Nutrition facts Nutrition facts per serving:

Calories 381; Fat 26.9g; Sodium 450mg; Carbs 14.2g; Protein 24g

PROSCIUTTO AND CHEESE EGGS

More like a formula than a recipe, switching up ingredients in a bake makes a little different and life easier. It is easy to swap cheeses for others, milk, and other ingredients as well. Just make sure it is tasty.

Preparation Time: 5 minutes | Cooking Time: 25 minutes | Servings: 4

Ingredients

4 eggs, beaten

1 cup milk

1 orange bell pepper, seeded and chopped

1 teaspoon pink salt

1 teaspoon ground black pepper

1 cup shredded Monterey Jack cheese

8 ounces prosciutto, chopped

1 cup water

Directions

1. In a bowl, put the almond milk, eggs, pink salt, and black pepper and whisk until evenly combined and a creamy color has formed. Stir in the Monterey Jack Cheese.

2. Arrange the bell pepper and prosciutto onto a baking dish. Then, pour over the egg mixture, cover the pan with aluminum foil and put on the reversible rack.

3. Add the water into the pot, put the rack with the dish in the pot.

4. Then, seal the pressure lid, choose Pressure and set to High. Set the time to 20 minutes. Choose Start/Stop.

5. When done cooking, perform a quick pressure release and carefully remove the lid. Take out the dish from the pot and place it on a cooling rack. Cool for 5 minutes and serve.

Nutrition facts Nutrition facts per serving:

Calories 332; Fat 21g; Sodium 1693mg; Carbs 6g; Protein 28g

PANCETTA HASH BROWNS

Hash browns are meant to be crispy, crunchy, and tasty. So, no room for soggy turnips. Making them with all these qualities never got better with the Multicooker. While tastes are well blended, also expect a beauty on your table from crispy pancetta, well-baked eggs, and crunchy hash browns.

Preparation Time: 10 minutes | Cooking Time: 30 minutes | Servings: 3

Ingredients

5 slices pancetta, chopped

1 white onion, diced

2 potatoes, peeled and grated

1 teaspoon sweet paprika

1 teaspoon pink salt

1 teaspoon ground black pepper

1 teaspoon garlic powder

3 eggs

Directions

1. Choose Sear/Sauté and set to High to preheat your cooker. Place in the pancetta and cook for 5 minutes, or until crispy.
2. Stir in the onion, potatoes, eggs, the sweet paprika, pink salt, black pepper, and garlic powder. Press the hash brown mixture.
3. Close the crisping lid, choose Bake/Roast and cook for 25 minutes at 350 degrees F.
4. Once the timer goes off, ensure the hash brown is perfectly golden brown on top. Serve immediately.

Nutrition facts Nutrition facts per serving:

Calories 364; Fat 24g; Sodium 1008mg; Carbs 24g; Protein 14g

EASY TOMATO-BASIL DIP

One more dip for you to add to your collection of dips for all your tasty veggie bites. Basil is full amazing aromas, I never get tired of it and sometimes I wish I could use it for everything, however, in this dip it proves itself to be in the high ranks of aromatic herbs.

Preparation Time: 5 minutes | Cooking Time: 13 minutes | Servings: 6

Ingredients:

1 cup chopped Tomatoes

¼ cup chopped Basil

10 oz shredded Parmesan Cheese

10 oz Cream Cheese

½ cup Heavy Cream

1 cup Water

Directions:

1. Open the cooker and pour in the tomatoes, basil, heavy cream, cream cheese, and water.
2. Close the lid, secure the pressure valve, and select Pressure for 3 minutes at High. Press Start/Stop.
3. Once the timer has ended, do a natural pressure release for 10 minutes.
4. Stir the mixture with a spoon while mashing the tomatoes with the back of the spoon. Add the parmesan cheese and Close the crisping lid.
5. Select Bake/Roast mode, set the temperature to 370 F and the time to 3 minutes.
6. Dish the dip into a bowl and serve with chips or veggie bites.

Nutrition facts Nutrition facts per serving:

Calories 350; Fat 28g; Sodium 120mg; Carbs 10g; Protein 13g

PARTY EGG BRULEE

Instead of waiting for dinner and then having a crème brulee as dessert, you can make this egg version to be snacked on during your working hours. It is really simple and you can even teach the little ones that are good enough with an appliance to make them for themselves.

Preparation Time: 2 minutes | Cooking Time: 10 minutes | Servings: 8

Ingredients:

8 large Eggs

1 tsp Sugar

Salt to taste

1 cup Water

Ice Bath

Directions:

1. Open the cooker, pour the water in, and fit the reversible rack in it. Put the eggs on the rack in a single layer, close the lid, secure the pressure valve, and select Pressure on High Pressure for 5 minutes. Press Start/Stop. Once the timer has ended, do a quick pressure release, and open the pot.

2. Remove the eggs into the ice bath and peel the eggs. Put the peeled eggs in a plate and slice them in half.

3. Sprinkle a bit of salt on them and then followed by the sugar. Lay onto your crisp basket fryer basket. Select Air Crisp mode, set the temperature to 390 degrees F and the time to 3 minutes.

Nutrition facts Nutrition facts per serving:

Calories 77; Fat 5.3g; Sodium 139mg; Carbs 1g; Protein 7.3g

BACON WRAPPED CHEESE BOMBS

Just 3 ingredients and you should have something creamy and tasty to munch on anytime. These bacon bombs are not fattening so you have as much as you want.

Preparation Time: 10 minutes | Cooking Time: 10 minutes | Servings: 8

Ingredients:

8 Bacon Slices, cut in half

3 tbsp Butter, melted

16 oz Mozzarella Cheese, cut into 8 pieces

Directions:

1. Wrap each cheese string with a slice of bacon and secure the ends with toothpicks. Set aside.

2. Grease the crisp basket with the melted butter and add in the bombs. Close the crisping lid, select Air Crisp mode, and set the temperature to 370 degrees F and set the time to 10 minutes.

3. At the 5-minute mark, turn the bombs. When ready, remove to a paper-lined plate to drain the excess oil. Serve on a platter with toothpicks and tomato dip.

Nutrition facts Nutrition facts per serving:

Calories 230; Fat 13.5g; Sodium 310mg; Carbs 2g; Protein 24g

CRUNCHY BACON CHEESEBURGER DIP

Need something to make chips tastier, then you should make this dip. The sound of bacon in a blend of cheese is mouthwatering already, and I think I might get this whooped up in a short while. Support the ideas? Do it too!

Preparation Time: 5 minutes | Cooking Time: 5 minutes | Servings: 10

Ingredients:

½ cup chopped Tomatoes

10 oz shredded Monterey Jack Cheese

10 oz Cream Cheese

10 Bacon Slices, chopped roughly

1 cup Water

Directions:

1. Turn on the cooker and select Air Crisp mode. Set the temperature to 370 degrees F and the time to 8 minutes.
2. Add the bacon pieces and close the crisping lid. Press Start/Stop.
3. When ready, open the lid and add the water, cream cheese, and tomatoes. Do Not Stir.
4. Close the lid, secure the pressure valve, and select Pressure mode on High for 5 minutes. Press Start/Stop.
5. Once the timer has ended, do a quick pressure release, and open the lid.
6. Stir in the cheddar cheese and mix to combine. Serve with a side of chips.

Nutrition facts Nutrition facts per serving:

Calories 353; Fat 25.3g; Sodium 88mg; Carbs 20.5g; Protein 7.9g

HONEY-MUSTARD SAUSAGE WEENIES

Party food, appetizer or mid-day snack, these weenies are delicious and will go round with many requests for more.

Preparation Time: 15 minutes | Cooking Time: 7 minutes | Servings: 4

Ingredients:

20 Hot Dogs, cut into 4 pieces

Salt and Black Pepper to taste

1 tsp Dijon Mustard

1 ½ tsp Soy Sauce

¼ cup Honey

¼ cup Red Wine Vinegar

½ cup Tomato Puree

¼ cup Water

Directions:

1. Add the tomato puree, red wine vinegar, honey, soy sauce, Dijon mustard, salt, and black pepper in a medium bowl. Mix them with a spoon.
2. Put sausage weenies in the crisp basket, and close the crisping lid.
3. Select Air Crisp mode. Set the temperature to 370 degrees F and the timer to 4 minutes. Press Start/Stop. At the 2-minute mark, turn the sausages.
4. Once ready, open the lid and pour the sweet sauce over the sausage weenies.
5. Close the pressure lid, secure the pressure valve, and select Pressure mode on High for 3 minutes. Press Start/Stop.
6. Once the timer has ended, do a quick pressure release. Serve and enjoy.

Nutrition facts Nutrition facts per serving:

Calories 180; Fat 15g; Sodium 170mg; Carbs 14g; Protein 10g

CHEESY CHICKEN DIP

Use this dip for all your veggie bites and the creamy effect will linger down your throat for hours. It is very straight forwarded to make, that's one reason why I love it!

Preparation Time: 3 minutes | Cooking Time: 1 hour 15 minutes | Servings: 6

Ingredients:

1 lb Chicken Breast
½ cup Breadcrumbs
10 oz Cheddar Cheese

½ cup Sour Cream
10 oz Cream Cheese
½ cup Water

Directions:

1. Open the cooker and add the chicken, water, and cream cheese.
2. Close the lid, secure the pressure valve, and select Pressure mode on High for 10 minutes. Press Start/Stop.
3. Once the timer has ended, do a quick pressure release, and open the pot.
4. Add the cheddar cheese and shred the chicken with two forks. Sprinkle with breadcrumbs, and close the crisping lid. Select Bake/Roast, set the temperature to 380 degrees F and the timer to 3 minutes.
5. Serve warm with veggie bites.

Nutrition facts Nutrition facts per serving:

Calories 387; Fat 26g; Sodium 302mg; Carbs 10.2g; Protein 27g

CINNAMON OATMEAL WITH CRANBERRIES

Isn't oatmeal more enjoyable when made faster? Right, that it is how fast it cooks here. A more nutritious version to regular oatmeal, I make them with some chia seeds oatmeal and then enhanced the dish with some raspberries. It is a quick one for me so I can get to work in good spirit.

Preparation Time: 5 minutes | Cooking Time: 10 minutes | Servings: 4

Ingredients

2 cups old-fashioned oatmeal

¼ cup plain vinegar

½ teaspoon nutmeg powder

1 tablespoon cinnamon powder

½ teaspoon vanilla extract

3¾ cups water

½ cup dried cranberries, plus more for garnish

2 raspberries, sliced

⅛ teaspoon salt

Honey, for topping

Directions

1. Combine the oatmeal, water, vinegar, nutmeg, cinnamon, vanilla, cranberries, and salt in the pot. Seal the pressure lid, choose Pressure mode and cook for 10 minutes on High. Press Start/Stop.

2. When the timer has ended, perform a natural pressure release for 10 minutes, then carefully open the lid.

3. Stir the oatmeal, drizzle with honey and decorate with raspberries. Serve immediately.

Nutrition facts Nutrition facts per serving:

Calories 399; Fat 6g; Sodium 76mg; Carbs 71g; Protein 14g

POACHED EGGS ON HEIRLOOM RIPE TOMATOES

You almost can't tear poached eggs away from brunch because they are always the perfect items to have. Now, you do not need to worry about disappointments from the stove top, just set the Multicooker right and your brunch table will be beaming with goodness.

Preparation Time: 7 minutes | Cooking Time: 3 minutes | Servings: 4

Ingredients:

4 large Eggs

1 cup Water

2 large Heirloom Ripe Tomatoes, halved crosswise

Salt and Black Pepper to taste

1 tsp chopped Fresh Herbs, of your choice

2 tbsp grated Parmesan Cheese

Cooking Spray

Directions:

1. Pour the water into the cooker and fit the reversible rack.
2. Grease the ramekins with the cooking spray and crack each egg into them.
3. Season with salt and pepper. Cover the ramekins with aluminum foil.
4. Place the cups on the trivet. Seal the lid.
5. Select Steam mode for 3 minutes on High pressure. Press Start/Stop.
6. Once the timer goes off, do a quick pressure release.
7. Use a napkin to remove the ramekins onto a flat surface.
8. In serving plates, share the halved tomatoes and toss the eggs in the ramekin over on each tomato half.
9. Sprinkle with salt and pepper, parmesan, and garnish with chopped herbs.

Nutrition facts Nutrition facts per serving:

Calories 123; Fat 6.9g; Sodium 147mg; Carbs 7.6g; Protein 6.3g

TASTY GIANT PANCAKE

You know how pancakes are often flat and boring sometimes, how about a bit of tweak up? This pancake is compacted with goodness and melts in your mouth at every bite. Drizzle some monk fruit syrup on it and enjoy this world of nourishment.

Preparation Time: 15 minutes | Cooking Time: 15 minutes | Servings: 6

Ingredients:

3 cups All-purpose Flour

¾ cup Sugar

5 Eggs

⅓ cup Olive Oil

⅓ cup Sparkling Water

⅓ tsp Salt

1 ½ tsp Baking Soda

2 tbsp Maple Syrup

A dollop of Whipped Cream to serve

Directions:

1. Start by pouring the flour, sugar, eggs, olive oil, sparkling water, salt, and baking soda into a food processor and blend until smooth.
2. Pour the batter into the cooker and let it sit in there for 15 minutes. Close the lid and secure the pressure valve.
3. Select the Pressure mode on Low pressure for 10 minutes. Press Start/Stop.
4. Once the timer goes off, press Start/Stop, quick-release the pressure valve to let out any steam and open the lid.
5. Gently run a spatula around the pancake to let loose any sticking.
6. Once ready, slide the pancake onto a serving plate and drizzle with maple syrup. Top with the whipped cream to serve.

Nutrition facts Nutrition facts per serving:

Calories 432; Fat 15.6g; Sodium 133mg; Carbs 59.1g; Protein 11.3g

CHICKEN

WHOLE ROASTED CHICKEN WITH WHITE WINE AND ROSEMARY

Roasting chicken regularly isn't for the faint. The thought of prepping up a full chicken is enough to discourage you. However, with the cooker, of course, you are up for quick, moist, tender, and tasty chicken.

Preparation Time: 10 minutes | Cooking Time: 30 minutes | Servings: 4

Ingredients

4-pound whole chicken

½ cup white wine

Juice of 1 lemon

2 limes, juiced

3 tbsp olive oil

¼ cup coconut aminos

1 tbsp ground cumin

6 cloves garlic, grated

1 tablespoon salt

3 tbsp chopped fresh rosemary

Directions

1. Rinse the chicken thoroughly with water and tie the legs with butcher's twine.
2. Pour the wine and lemon juice into the pot. Place the chicken in the Cook & Crisp basket and fix the basket in the higher position of the pot.
3. Seal the pressure lid, choose Pressure and set to High. Set the time to 20 minutes, then Choose Start/Stop. When the timer is done, perform a quick pressure release, and carefully open the lid.
4. In a bowl, combine the lime juice, the olive oil, coconut aminos, cumin, garlic, and salt; mix until thoroughly combined. Brush the mixture over the chicken.
5. Close the crisping lid, choose Air Crisp, set the temperature to 390 degrees F, and set the time to 15 minutes. Choose Start/Stop.
6. After about 10 minutes, lift the crisping lid and sprinkle the chicken with the fresh rosemary. Close the Lid and continue cooking.
7. When the timer rings, transfer the chicken to a plate
8. Let the chicken rest for 10 minutes before cutting and serving.

Nutrition facts Nutrition facts per serving:

Calories: 418; Fat: 30g; Sodium: 1845mg; Carbohydrates: 2g; Protein: 31g

CRISPY CHICKEN WITH QUINOA AND THYME CARROTS

Chicken thighs are everything that we love in my home; they are very affordable and bursting with so much flavor. In this recipe, I use skin-on and bone-in chicken thighs because they are tastier. Cooking them in pressure keeps them moist and soft. After, I roast some carrots with the crisping lid along with the crackling flavorful chicken skin.

Preparation Time: 10 minutes | Cooking Time: 12 minutes | Servings: 4

Ingredients

1½ cups chicken broth

1 cup quinoa

4 bone-in, skin-on chicken thighs

2 carrots, chopped

2 tbsp melted butter

2 tsp chicken seasoning

1 tsp salt, divided

2 tbsp chopped fresh thyme

Directions

1. Pour the chicken broth and quinoa in the pot.
2. Then, put in the reversible rack. Arrange the chicken thighs on the rack, skin side up, and arrange the carrots around the chicken.
3. Seal the pressure lid, choose Pressure, set to High, and the time to 2 minutes. Press Start/Stop.
4. When done cooking, perform a quick pressure release, and open the lid.
5. Brush the carrots and chicken with the melted butter. Season the chicken with the chicken seasoning and half of the salt. Also, season the carrots with the thyme and remaining salt.
6. Close the crisping lid, choose Broil and set the time to 10 minutes. Choose Start/Stop.
7. When done cooking, check for your desired crispiness, and the turn the Multicooker off.
8. Spoon the quinoa into serving plates, and serve the chicken and carrots over the rice.

Nutrition facts Nutrition facts per serving:

Calories: 425; Fat: 18g; Sodium: 761mg; Carbs: 48g; Protein: 18g

CHICKEN AND WILD RICE TACO BOWLS

So right here is a cookbook that champions tacos anytime of the year. This dish is a blend of faux carbs, proteins, and lip licking tastes. Get ready to be bugged for more!

Preparation Time: 4 minutes | Cooking Time: 25 minutes | Servings: 4

Ingredients:

4 Chicken Breasts

2 cups Chicken Broth

2 ¼ packets Taco Seasoning

1 cup Wild Rice, rinsed

1 Green Bell Pepper, seeded and diced

1 Red Bell Pepper, seeded and diced

1 cup Salsa

Salt and Black Pepper to taste

Sour Cream

To Serve:

Grated Cheese, of your choice

Chopped Cilantro

Avocado Slices

Directions:

1. Pour the chicken broth into the inner pot, add the chicken. Pour the taco seasoning over. Add the salsa and stir lightly with a spoon.
2. Close the pressure lid, secure the pressure valve, and select Pressure on High for 15 minutes. Press Start/Stop.
3. Once the timer has ended, do a quick pressure release, and open the lid.
4. Add the wild rice and peppers, and use a spoon to push them into the sauce.
5. Close the pressure lid, secure the pressure valve, and select Pressure mode on High for 8 minutes. Press Start/Stop.
6. Once the timer has ended, do a quick pressure release, and open the lid. Gently stir the mixture, adjust the taste with salt and pepper.
7. Stir in sour cream, close the crisping lid and select Broil mode; cook for 2 minutes.
8. Spoon the chicken dish into serving bowls. Top it with avocado slices, sprinkle with chopped cilantro and some cheese. Serve.

Nutrition facts Nutrition facts per serving:

Calories 523; Fat 22g; Sodium 540mg; Carbs 41g; Protein 44g

MUSHROOM CHICKEN FRIED RICE

We love fried rice as a family, but no one really wants to work with many pots and pans, talk less about cleaning them after cooking. This cooker makes things easier, faster, and less fussy because everything cooks in one pot. I look forward to many days of having fried rice and of course with tasty chicken.

Preparation Time: 5 minutes | Cooking Time: 20 minutes | Servings: 4

Ingredients

1 tbsp ghee

1 onion, diced

4 garlic cloves, minced

1 lb boneless, skinless chicken breasts

Salt and black pepper, to taste

2 cups chicken broth

¼ cup coconut aminos

1 cup long grain rice

16 ounces frozen mixed mushrooms

Directions

1. Choose Sear/Sauté on the pot and melt the ghee; sauté the onion for 5 minutes. Add garlic and cook until fragrant, about 1 minute.
2. Season the chicken with salt and black pepper and place in the pot and. Cook for 5 minutes until browned.
3. Pour in the chicken broth, coconut aminos, and rice.
4. Seal the pressure lid, choose Pressure, set to High, and set the time to 3 minutes. Press Start/Stop.
5. When the timer is done, perform a quick pressure and carefully open the lid.
6. Pour the frozen mushrooms into the pot. Choose Sear/Sauté and set to High. Choose Start/Stop. Cook for 5 minutes while stirring occasionally.
7. When ready, dish the fried rice with chicken and serve.

Nutrition facts Nutrition facts per serving:

Calories: 461; Fat: 7g; Sodium: 1305mg; Carbs: 60g; Protein: 38g

BEAN AND CHICKEN ENCHILADA

Right from childhood, I have always loved chicken enchiladas. Maybe it had to do with the way my mum made them; there was something special about those bites, and until this day, it is one of my favorite delicacies. Here, I try to make it as close to mother's so I make them cheesy and creamy.

Preparation Time: 10 minutes | Cooking Time: 20 minutes | Servings: 6

Ingredients

1 tbsp butter

1 yellow onion, diced

2 garlic cloves, minced

1 lb boneless, skinless chicken breasts

2 cups enchilada sauce

Salt and ground black pepper, to taste

15 oz canned pinto beans, drained and rinsed

8 tortillas, each cut into 8 pieces

1 cup frozen corn

2 cups shredded Monterey Jack cheese

Directions

1. Choose Sear/Sauté on the pot and melt the butter. Cook the onion for 5 minutes in the butter, stirring occasionally. Stir in the garlic and cook until fragrant, about 1 minute more.

2. Put the chicken and enchilada sauce in the pot, and season with salt and black pepper. Stir to combine.

3. Seal the pressure lid, choose Pressure, set to High, and set the time to 15 minutes. Press Start/Stop.

4. When done cooking, perform a quick pressure release and carefully open the lid.

5. Shred the chicken with two forks. Mix in the pinto beans, tortilla pieces, corn, and cheese.

6. Close the crisping lid, choose Broil and set the time to 5 minutes. Press Start/Stop.

7. When ready, allow sitting for 5 minutes before serving.

Nutrition facts Nutrition facts per serving:

Calories: 511; Fat: 17g; Sodium: 1081mg; Carbs: 54g; Protein: 38g

COQ AU VIN

An exceptional French delicacy which cooks perfectly in the Multicooker. It is a good option when you have visitors coming; however, you'll have to plan some hours ahead to get the tastes and flavors right. Your guest will love your home because of this dish.

Preparation Time: 8 h 10 minutes | Cooking Time: 50 minutes | Servings: 4

Ingredients:

3 Chicken Legs, cut into drumsticks and thighs

2 Bacon Slices, chopped

1 ½ cups Dry White Wine

Salt and Black Pepper to taste+

½ bunch Thyme, divided

8 oz Shiitake Mushrooms, stems removed

and cut into 4 pieces

3 Shallots, peeled

3 tbsp Butter, divided

3 skinny Carrots, cut into pieces

2 cloves Garlic, crushed

1 tbsp All-purpose flour

3 tbsp chopped Parsley for garnishing

Directions:

1. Put the chicken on a clean flat surface and season on both sides with salt and pepper. In a plastic zipper bag, pour the wine.

2. Add half of the thyme and chicken. Zip the bag and shake to coat the chicken well with the wine. Place it in the refrigerator for 6 to 8 hours.

3. After 8 hours, turn on the cooker on High and fry the bacon on Sear/Sauté mode for about 8 minutes. Remove the bacon without the fat onto a plate using a slotted spoon. Set aside.

4. Pour the mushroom into the pot, season with salt and cook for 5 minutes. Then, remove at the side of the bacon.

5. Remove the chicken from the refrigerator onto a clean flat surface. Take out and discard the thyme but reserve the marinade. Pat the chicken dry with paper towels.

6. Melt half of the butter in the pot on Sauté. Place the chicken in the butter in batches and fry until dark golden brown on each side, about 12 minutes.

7. Add bacon, mushrooms, shallots, garlic, carrots, and a bit of salt. Cook the ingredients for 4 minutes and top with the wine and remaining thyme.

8. Close the pressure lid, secure the pressure valve, and select Pressure mode on High for 15 minutes. Press Start/Stop.

9. Meanwhile, add the flour and the remaining butter in a bowl, and smash them together with a fork. Set aside. Once the timer has ended, do a natural pressure release for 10 minutes.

10. Discard the thyme. Add the flour mixture to the sauce in the pot, stir until well incorporated. Adjust the seasoning with salt and black pepper.

11. Close the crisping lid and select Broil mode. Cook for 4 minutes. Press Start.

12. Garnish with parsley and serve with steamed asparagus.

Nutrition facts Nutrition facts per serving:

Calories 422; Fat 22g; Sodium 440mg; Carbs 15.2g; Protein 32g

CLASSIC TUSCAN CHICKEN

I can't get enough of Tuscan chicken on a lazy Saturday afternoon. It is filling while light for the body to help me drag my feet around in style. I like to add some more pepper flakes to it when I'm in the mood to feel high.

Preparation Time: 10 minutes | Cooking Time: 20 minutes | Servings: 4

Ingredients:

4 Chicken Thighs, cut into 1-inch pieces	2 tbsp Italian Seasoning
1 tbsp Olive Oil	2 cups Baby Spinach
1 ½ cups Chicken Broth	¼ tsp Red Pepper Flakes
Salt to taste	6 oz softened Cream Cheese, cubed
10 chopped Sun-Dried Tomatoes with Herbs	1 cup shredded Pecorino Cheese

Directions:

1. Pour the chicken broth into the pressure cooker, and add the Italian seasoning, chicken, tomatoes, salt, and red pepper flakes. Stir with a spoon.

2. Close the lid, secure the pressure valve, and select Pressure mode on High for 12 minutes. Press Start/Stop.

3. Once the timer has ended, do a quick pressure release, and open the lid.

4. Add and stir in the spinach, parmesan cheese, and cream cheese until the cheese melts and is fully incorporated.

5. Close the crisping lid and cook on Broil mode for 5 minutes.

6. Dish the chicken over a bed of zoodles or a side of steamed asparagus.

Nutrition facts Nutrition facts per serving:

Calories 576; Fat 44g; Sodium 245mg; Carbs 12g; Protein 45g

ITALIAN-STYLE LEMON CHICKEN

Zingy goodness! This one pot chicken dish is full of life. The lemon added has a magical way of kicking those happy moods up while keeping your body in the healthiest states possible. Serve these chicken pieces with a side of steamed spinach and kale mix and drizzle the sauce from it all over the dish. You will love it!

Preparation Time: 5 minutes | Cooking Time: 21 minutes | Servings: 4

Ingredients:

4 Chicken Thighs

1 ½ tbsp Olive Oil

½ tsp Garlic Powder

Salt and Black Pepper to taste

½ tsp Red Pepper Flakes

½ tsp Smoked Paprika

1 small Onion, chopped

2 cloves Garlic, sliced

½ cup Chicken Broth

1 tsp Italian Seasoning

1 Lemon, zested and juiced

1 ½ tbsp Heavy Cream

Lemon slices to garnish

Chopped parsley to garnish

Directions:

1. Preheat the cooker by selecting Sear/Sauté mode on Medium. Warm the olive oil and add the chicken thighs; cook to brown on each side for about 3 minutes. Remove the browned chicken onto a plate.

2. Melt the butter in the pot, then, add garlic, onions, and lemon juice. Deglaze the bottom of the pot and cook for 1 minute. Add the Italian seasoning, chicken broth, lemon zest, and the chicken.

3. Close the pressure lid, secure the pressure valve, select Pressure mode on High for 10 minutes. Press Start/Stop.

4. When ready, do a quick pressure release. Open the lid. Stir in the heavy cream. Close the crisping lid and select Broil mode. Set the time to 5 minutes. Serve with the steamed kale and spinach mix. Garnish with the lemons slices and parsley.

Nutrition facts Nutrition facts per serving:

Calories 487; Fat 36g; Sodium 268mg; Carbs 8g; Protein 28g

CREAMY CHICKEN BREASTS WITH BASIL PESTO

Can we ever get tired of tasty creamy dishes? Not me I'm sure. This cream infused chicken dish is not only tasty but very healthy for most dieting needs. I love it when the children splurge over it on noodles, but for me, I enjoy it over a mix of spiralized vegetables.

Preparation Time: 3 minutes | Cooking Time: 20 minutes | Servings: 4

Ingredients:

4 Chicken Breasts, skinless and boneless
½ cup Heavy Cream
½ cup Chicken Broth
⅓ tsp minced Garlic
Salt and Black Pepper to taste

⅓ tsp Italian Seasoning
¼ cup Roasted Red Peppers
1 tbsp Basil Pesto
1 tbsp Cornstarch

Directions:

1. In the inner pot of the cooker, add the chicken at the bottom. Pour the chicken broth and add Italian seasoning, garlic, salt, and pepper.
2. Close the pressure lid, secure the pressure valve, and select Pressure mode on High for 15 minutes. Press Start/Stop.
3. Once the timer has ended, do a natural pressure release for 5 minutes and open the lid.
4. Use a spoon to remove the chicken onto a plate. Scoop out any fat or unwanted chunks from the sauce.
5. In a small bowl, add the cream, cornstarch, red peppers, and pesto. Mix them with a spoon. Pour the creamy mixture into the pot and close the crisping lid.
6. Select Broil mode and cook for 4 minutes.
7. Serve the chicken with sauce over on a bed of cooked quinoa.

Nutrition facts Nutrition facts per serving:

Calories 372; Fat 19g; Sodium 497mg; Carbs 5g; Protein 35g

SPICY-SWEET SHREDDED CHICKEN

Ok, so having a Multicooker and not making some sweet, spicy chicken already will be under-utilizing your pot. This dish is mild on flavor but has that spicy kick to set you active the rest of the day hence the best time to have this sauce is at lunch.

Preparation Time: 7 minutes | Cooking Time: 28 minutes | Servings: 4

Ingredients:

4 Chicken Breasts, skinless

¼ cup Sriracha Sauce

2 tbsp Butter

1 tsp grated Ginger

2 cloves Garlic, minced

½ tsp Cayenne Pepper

½ tsp Red Chili Flakes

½ cup Honey

½ cup Chicken Broth

Salt and Black Pepper to taste

Chopped Scallion to garnish

Directions:

1. In a bowl, pour the chicken broth. Mix in honey, ginger, sriracha sauce, red pepper flakes, cayenne pepper, and garlic. Set aside.
2. Put the chicken on a plate and season with salt and pepper. Set aside too. Select Sear/Sauté mode on High on your cooker.
3. Melt the butter, and add the chicken in 2 batches to brown on both sides for about 3 minutes. Add the chicken back, and pour the pepper sauce over.
4. Close the pressure lid, secure the pressure valve, and select Pressure mode on High for 20 minutes. Press Start/Stop.
5. When ready, do a natural pressure release for 5 minutes and open the lid. Remove the chicken onto a cutting board and shred using two forks.
6. Return the shredded chicken to the pot, close the crisping lid and Select Air Crisp mode. Adjust the time to 4 minutes at 385 degrees F.
7. When ready, transfer the chicken to a serving bowl, pour the sauce over, and garnish with the scallions.
8. Serve with a side of sautéed mushrooms.

Nutrition facts Nutrition facts per serving:

Calories 462; Fat 16g; Sodium 540mg; Carbs 38g; Protein 37g

CHICKEN & BACON NOODLE SOUP

If you are looking for something that is in between light and filling for lunch, this chicken turnip soup has you in the right place. This recipe is a good way to combine carbs with some fats and proteins for a more tummy filling desire.

Preparation Time: 10 minutes | Cooking Time: 23 minutes | Servings: 8

Ingredients:

5 oz dry Egg Noodles

4 Chicken Breasts, skinless and boneless

1 large White Onion, chopped

8 Bacon Slices, chopped

4 cloves Garlic, minced

Salt and Black Pepper to taste

2 medium Carrots, sliced

2 cups sliced Celery

½ cup chopped Parsley

1 ½ tsp Dried Thyme

8 cups Chicken Broth

Directions:

1. Turn on the cooker, and select Sear/Sauté mode on High. Press Start. Add the chopped bacon and fry for 5 minutes until nicely brown and crispy.

2. Remove to a paper towel to soak up excess oil and set aside.

3. Add the onion and garlic to the pot and cook for 3 minutes until tender. Add the chicken breasts, noodles, carrots, celery, chicken broth, thyme, salt, and pepper.

4. Close the pressure lid, secure the valve to seal, and select Pressure mode on High pressure. Adjust the time to 5 minutes and press Start/Stop.

5. Once the timer has ended, do a quick pressure release, and open the lid. Use a wooden spoon to remove the chicken onto a plate. Shred the chicken with two forks and add it back to the soup.

6. Stir in the bacon. Adjust the seasoning as desired. Close the crisping lid and cook on Broil mode for 5 minutes. Adjust the seasoning.

7. Ladle the soup into serving bowls and serve with a side of bread.

Nutrition facts Nutrition facts per serving:

Calories 419; Fat 19g; Sodium 640mg; Carbs 15.3g; Protein 35g

BUFFALO CHICKEN SOUP

This soup is creamy, full of sharp flavor, and very VERY satisfying.

Preparation Time: 7 minutes | Cooking Time: 30 minutes | Servings: 4

Ingredients:

4 Chicken Breasts, boneless and skinless

½ cup Hot Sauce

2 large White Onion, finely chopped

2 cups finely chopped Celery

1 tbsp Olive Oil

1 tsp dried Thyme

3 cups Chicken Broth

1 tsp Garlic Powder

½ cup crumbled Blue Cheese + extra for serving

4 oz Cream Cheese, cubed in small pieces

Salt and Pepper, to taste

Directions:

1. Put the chicken on a clean flat surface and season with pepper and salt. Set aside. Select Sear/Sauté mode on High.

2. Heat in olive oil, add onion and celery. Sauté them, constant stirring, until they are nice and soft, for about 5 minutes.

3. Then, add garlic powder and thyme. Stir and cook for about a minute, and add the chicken, hot sauce, and chicken broth. Season with salt and pepper. Close the pressure lid, secure the pressure valve, and select Pressure mode on High for 15 minutes. Press Start/Stop.

4. Meanwhile, put the blue cheese and cream cheese in a bowl, and use a fork to smash them together. Set the resulting mixture aside.

5. Once the timer has ended, do a natural pressure release for 5 minutes. Take out the chicken on to a flat surface with a slotted spoon and use two forks to shred them. Return shredded chicken to the pot, close the crisping lid, select Broil mode and cook for 5 minutes.

6. Add the cheese to the pot and stir until is slightly incorporated into the sauce.

7. Dish the buffalo chicken soup into bowls. Sprinkle the remaining cheese over the soup and serve with sliced baguette.

Nutrition facts Nutrition facts per serving:

Calories 487; Fat 34.3g; Sodium 373mg; Carbs 8g; Protein 41g

GORGEOUS CHICKEN FAJITAS WITH GUACAMOLE

These chicken fajitas are made to be rich in flavor, so you enjoy the aroma that exudes from every ingredient. It is essential to use corn tacos else you'll be breaking the deliciousness rule. Make as much as you can and share. It is effortless to do.

Preparation Time: 10 minutes | Cooking Time: 20 minutes | Servings: 4

Ingredients:

2 lb Chicken Breasts, skinless and cut in 1-inch slices

½ cup Chicken Broth

1 Yellow Onion, sliced

1 Green Bell Pepper, seeded and sliced

1 Yellow Bell Pepper, seeded and sliced

1 Red Bell Pepper, seeded and sliced

2 tbsp Cumin Powder

2 tbsp Chili Powder

Salt to taste

Half a Lime

Cooking Spray

Fresh cilantro, to garnish

Assembling:

Tacos, Guacamole, Sour Cream, Salsa, Cheese

Directions:

1. Grease the inner pot with cooking spray and line the bottom with the peppers and onion. Lay the chicken on the bed of peppers.
2. Sprinkle with salt, chili powder, and cumin powder. Squeeze some lime juice and pour in chicken broth. Close the lid, secure the pressure valve, and select Pressure mode on High pressure for 15 minutes. Press Start/Stop.
3. Once the timer has ended, do a quick pressure release, and open the lid.
4. Close the crisping lid and cook for 5 minutes on Bake/Roast mode at 370 F.
5. Dish the chicken with the vegetables and juice onto a large serving platter.
6. Add sour cream, cheese, guacamole, salsa, and tacos in one layer on the side of the chicken.

Nutrition facts Nutrition facts per serving:

Calories 423; Fat 22.1g; Sodium 479mg; Carbs 9g; Protein 39.7g

MEDITERRANEAN MEATBALLS PRIMAVERA

Sometimes, meatballs are just what you need to boost your mood up. Make this easy meatball dish that goes with many types of sauces and vegetable sides. You can make some extra pieces and refrigerate them for a weekly meal pack.

Preparation Time: 10 minutes | Cooking Time: 20 minutes | Servings: 4

Ingredients:

1 lb Ground Chicken

1 Egg, cracked into a bowl

6 tsp Flour

Salt and Black Pepper to taste

2 tbsp chopped Basil + Extra to garnish

1 tbsp Olive Oil + ½ tbsp Olive Oil

1 ½ tsp Italian Seasoning

1 Red Bell Pepper, seeded and sliced

2 cups chopped Green Beans

½ lb chopped Asparagus

1 cup chopped Tomatoes

1 cup Chicken Broth

Directions:

1. In a mixing bowl, add the chicken, egg, flour, salt, pepper, 2 tablespoons of basil, 1 tablespoon of olive oil, and Italian seasoning. Mix them well with hands and make 16 large balls out of the mixture. Set the meatballs aside.

2. Select Sear/Sauté mode. Heat half teaspoon of olive oil, and add peppers, green beans, and asparagus. Cook for 3 minutes, stirring frequently.

3. After 3 minutes, use a spoon the veggies onto a plate and set aside.

4. Pour the remaining oil in the pot to heat and then fry the meatballs in it in batches. Fry them for 2 minutes on each side to brown them lightly.

5. After, put all the meatballs back into the pot as well as the vegetables. Also, pour the chicken broth over it.

6. Close the lid, secure the pressure valve, and select Pressure mode on High pressure for 10 minutes. Press Start/Stop. Do a quick pressure release.

7. Close the crisping lid and select Air Crisp. Cook for 5 minutes at 400 degrees F, until nice and crispy.

8. Dish the meatballs with sauce into a serving bowl and garnish it with basil. Serve with overcooked tagliatelle pasta.

Nutrition facts Nutrition facts per serving:

Calories 378; Fat 19.2g; Sodium 340mg; Carbs 13g; Protein 26g

GREEK-STYLE STUFFED CHICKEN

Spinach feta stuffed chicken is something you can have on a special dinner when you are unsure of what to make. The spinach brings a worth of nutrients to the table while the feta cheese balances the taste of blandness from the spinach.

Preparation Time: 10 minutes | Cooking Time: 20 minutes | Servings: 4

Ingredients:

4 Chicken Breasts, skinless

Salt and Black Pepper to taste

1 cup Baby Spinach, frozen

½ cup crumbled Feta Cheese

½ tsp dried Oregano

½ tsp Garlic Powder

2 tbsp Olive Oil

2 tsp dried Parsley

1 cup Water

Directions:

1. Wrap the chicken in plastic and put on a cutting board. Use a rolling pin to pound flat to a quarter inch thickness. Remove the plastic wrap.
2. In a bowl, mix spinach, salt, and feta cheese and scoop the mixture onto the chicken breasts. Wrap the chicken to secure the spinach filling in it.
3. Use toothpicks to secure the wrap firmly from opening. Gently season the chicken pieces with oregano, parsley, garlic powder, and pepper.
4. Select Sear/Sauté mode on the cooker. Heat the oil, add the chicken, and sear to golden brown on each side. Work in 2 batches.
5. Remove the chicken onto a plate and set aside.
6. Pour the water into the pot and use a spoon to scrape the bottom of the pot to let loose any chicken pieces or seasoning that is stuck to the bottom of the pot. Fit the reversiblerack into the pot with care as the pot will still be hot.
7. Transfer the chicken onto the rack. Seal the lid and select Pressure mode on High pressure for 10 minutes. Press Start/Stop.
8. Once the timer has ended, do a quick pressure release. Close the crisping lid and cook on Bake/Roast mode for 5 minutes at 370 F. Plate the chicken and serve with a side of sautéed asparagus, and some slices of tomatoes.

Nutrition facts Nutrition facts per serving:

Calories 417; Fat 27g; Sodium 410mg; Carbs 3g; Protein 33g

CREAMY CHICKEN STEW WITH MUSHROOMS & SPINACH

The look of this dish will make your guests hungry in an instance. Figuring out what the best dinner stew should be when you have a few friends visiting? This is one perfect choice! Serve it to a side of buttery squash mash, and you'll be in awe at the taste.

Preparation Time: 25 minutes | Cooking Time: 31 minutes | Servings: 4

Ingredients:

4 Chicken Breasts, diced

1 ¼ lb White Button Mushrooms, halved

3 tbsp Olive Oil

1 large Onion, sliced

5 cloves Garlic, minced

Salt and Black Pepper to taste

1 ¼ tsp Cornstarch

½ cup Spinach, chopped

1 Bay Leaf

1 ½ cups Chicken Stock

1 tsp Dijon Mustard

1 ½ cup Sour Cream

3 tbsp Chopped Parsley

Directions:

1. Select Sear/Sauté mode and set to medium High to preheat.
2. Once the pot is ready, heat the olive oil then include the onion and sauté for 3 minutes until soft. Add the mushrooms, chicken, garlic, bay leaf, salt, pepper, Dijon mustard, and chicken broth. Stir well.
3. Close the lid, secure the pressure valve, and press Pressure mode on High pressure for 15 minutes. Press Start/Stop.
4. Once the timer has ended, do a natural pressure release for 5 minutes and carefully open the lid. Stir the stew, remove the bay leaf, and scoop some of the liquid into a bowl. Add the cornstarch to the liquid and mix them until completely lump free.
5. Pour the liquid into the sauce, stir it, and let the sauce thicken to your desired consistency. Top it with the sour cream, close the crisping lid and select Broil mode. Cook for 2 minutes.
6. Garnish with the chopped parsley and serve with steamed green peas.

Nutrition facts Nutrition facts per serving:

Calories 456; Fat 26.3g; Sodium 450mg; Carbs 22g; Protein 42.1g

STICKY BARBECUE DRUMETTES

It is football season every time, and some barbecued chicken will do you some good. Instead of starting a charcoal grill for some grilled chicken, how about this quicker way of making them using the Multicooker. They get ready in 24 minutes.

Preparation Time: 5 minutes | Cooking Time: 24 minutes | Servings: 4

Ingredients:

2 lb Chicken Drumettes, bone in and skin in

½ cup Chicken Broth

½ tsp Dry Mustard

½ tsp Sweet Paprika

½ tbsp. Cumin Powder

½ tsp Onion Powder

¼ tsp Cayenne Powder

Salt and Pepper, to taste

1 stick Butter, sliced in 5 to 7 pieces

BBQ Sauce to taste

Cooking Spray

Directions:

1. Pour the chicken broth into the inner pot of cooker P and insert the reversiblerack. In a zipper bag, pour in dry mustard, cumin powder, onion powder, cayenne powder, salt, and pepper.

2. Add the chicken, close the bag and shake to coat the chicken well with the spices. You can toss the chicken in the spices in batches too.

3. Then, remove the chicken from the bag and place on the rack. Spread the butter slices on the drumsticks. Close the lid, secure the pressure valve, and select Pressure mode on High pressure for 10 minutes. Press Start/Stop.

4. Once the timer has ended, do a quick pressure release, and open the lid.

5. Remove the chicken onto a clean flat surface like a cutting board and brush them with the barbecue sauce using the brush. Return to the rack and close the crisping lid.

6. Cook for 10 minutes at 400 F on Air Crisp mode. Serve immediately.

Nutrition facts Nutrition facts per serving:

Calories 374; Fat 11.3g; Sodium 262mg; Carbs 2.85g; Protein 38.3g

EASY CHICKEN THIGHS IN TOMATO SAUCE

You can call it a world passer simply because it works with so many kinds of dishes across continents and can be made just anywhere easily. Making it in the Multicooker is rewarding, so you get to save a lot of time for your work deadlines.

Preparation Time: 5 minutes | Cooking Time: 25 minutes | Servings: 4

Ingredients:

4 Chicken Thighs, skinless but with bone

4 tbsp Olive Oil

1 cup Crushed Tomatoes

1 large Red Bell Pepper, seeded and diced

1 large Green Bell Pepper, seeded and diced

1 Red Onion, diced

Salt and Black Pepper to taste

1 tbsp chopped Basil

½ cup Chicken Broth

1 bay Leaf

½ tsp dried Oregano

Directions:

1. Place the chicken on a clean flat surface and season with salt and pepper. Select Sear/Sauté mode on High, and heat the oil.
2. Once heated add the chicken to brown on both sides for 6 minutes. Then, add the onions and peppers. Cook for 5 minutes until nice and soft.
3. Add bay leaf, salt, broth, pepper, and oregano. Stir using a spoon. Close the pressure lid, secure the pressure valve, and select Pressure mode on High for 15 minutes. Press Start/Stop.
4. Once the timer has ended, do a natural pressure release for 5 minutes.
5. Discard the bay leaf. Stir in tomatoes, close the crisping lid, select Broil mode and cook for 25 minutes.
6. Dish the chicken with the sauce into a serving bowl and garnish with the chopped basil. Serve over a bed of steamed squash spaghetti.

Nutrition facts Nutrition facts per serving:

Calories 437; Fat 37g; Sodium 273mg; Carbs 8g; Protein 24g

COCONUT CHICKEN CURRY

You will love the color of this dish as it exudes excitement and healthiness. It cooks very fast, so this qualifies for a real hungry girl recipe. Make sure to use firm and fresh vegetables to give you the beautiful colors the dish should have as well as some crunch and fresh tastes.

Preparation Time: 12 minutes | Cooking Time: 20 minutes | Servings: 4

Ingredients:

4 Chicken Breasts

4 tbsp Red Curry Paste

½ cup Chicken Broth

2 cups Coconut Milk

4 tbsp Sugar

Salt and Black Pepper to taste

2 Red Bell Pepper, seeded and cut in 2-inch sliced

2 Yellow Bell Pepper, seeded and cut in 2-inch slices

2 cup Green Beans, cut in half

2 tbsp Lime Juice

Directions:

1. Add the chicken, red curry paste, salt, pepper, coconut milk, broth, and sugar, in the cooker inner pot.
2. Close the pressure lid, secure the pressure valve, and select Pressure mode on High for 15 minutes. Press Start/Stop.
3. Once the timer has ended, do a quick pressure release, and open the lid.
4. Remove the chicken onto a cutting board and close the crisping lid. Select Broil mode. Add the bell peppers, green beans, and lime juice.
5. Stir the sauce with a spoon and cook for 4 minutes. Slice the chicken with a knife, pour the sauce and vegetables over and serve warm.

Nutrition facts Nutrition facts per serving:

Calories 587; Fat 41g; Sodium 540mg; Carbs 30g; Protein 32g

BALSAMIC THYME CHICKEN THIGHS

Such a quick but taste-enhancing way to cook a chicken. This chicken dish is that kind you look forward to having after a hard day of work. It is rewarding of your efforts, and the whole family will dine well to it.

Preparation Time: 10 minutes | Cooking Time: 25 minutes | Servings: 4

Ingredients:

2 lb Chicken Thighs, bone in and skin on

2 tbsp Olive Oil

Salt and Pepper, to taste

1 ½ cups diced Tomatoes

¾ cup Yellow Onion

2 tsp minced Garlic

½ cup Balsamic Vinegar

3 tsp chopped fresh Thyme

1 cup Chicken Broth

2 tbsp chopped Parsley

Directions:

1. With paper towels, pat dry the chicken and season with salt and pepper.
2. Select Sear/Sauté mode. Warm the olive and add the chicken with skin side down. Cook to golden brown on each side, for about 9 minutes.
3. Remove onto a clean plate.
4. Then, add onions and tomatoes to the pot and sauté for 3 minutes, stirring occasionally with a spoon. Add in garlic and cook for 30 seconds, until fragrant.
5. Pour the chicken broth, and add some salt, thyme, and balsamic vinegar. Stir them using a spoon. Add the chicken back to the pot.
6. Close the lid, secure the pressure valve, and select Pressure mode on High pressure for 15 minutes. Press Start/Stop to start cooking.
7. When ready, do a quick pressure release.
8. Close the crisping lid and cook on Air Crisp mode for 5 minutes at 400 F.
9. Garnish with parsley and serve with thyme roasted tomatoes, carrots, and sweet potatoes.

Nutrition facts Nutrition facts per serving:

Calories 412; Fat 16g; Sodium 321mg; Carbs 13g; Protein 39g

HOLIDAY STUFFED FULL CHICKEN

Big size dinner soon? Get this zingy full chicken ready for the table in less than an hour. It is flavor packed and of course, very healthy and light to have in the evening.

Preparation Time: 4 minutes | Cooking Time: 47 minutes | Servings: 6

Ingredients:

4 lb Whole Chicken

1 tbsp Herbes de Provence Seasoning

1 tbsp Olive Oil

Salt and Black Pepper to season

2 cloves Garlic, peeled

1 tsp Garlic Powder

1 Yellow Onion, peeled and quartered

1 Lemon, quartered

1 ¼ cups Chicken Broth

Directions:

1. Put the chicken on a clean flat surface and pat dry using paper towels.
2. Sprinkle the top and cavity of the chicken with salt, black pepper, Herbes de Provence, and garlic powder.
3. Stuff the onion, lemon quarters, and garlic cloves into the cavity. In the cooker, fit the reversiblerack. Pour the broth in and place the chicken on the rack. Seal the lid, and select Pressure mode on High for 25 minutes.
4. Press Start/Stop to start cooking.
5. Once ready, do a natural pressure release for about 10 minutes, then a quick pressure release to let the remaining steam out, and press Stop.
6. Close the crisping lid and broil the chicken for 5 minutes on Broil mode, to ensure that it attains a golden brown color on each side.
7. Dish the chicken on a bed of steamed mixed veggies. Right here, the choice is yours to whip up some good veggies together as your appetite tells you.

Nutrition facts Nutrition facts per serving:

Calories 376; Fat 14g; Sodium 1040mg; Carbs 3g; Protein 53g

QUICK AND EASY CANNELLINI BEAN CHICKEN CHILI

Light and pretty to the eyes, this chicken chili goes well with any steamed vegetable dish. Make it for your lunch pack and the aromas from your bowl will earn you a lot of inquiries from your colleagues.

Preparation Time: 15 minutes | Cooking Time: 25 minutes | Servings: 4

Ingredients:

3 Chicken Breasts, cubed

3 cups Chicken Broth

1 tbsp Butter

1 White Onion, chopped

Salt and Black Pepper

2 (14.5 oz) cans Cannellini beans, drained

1 tsp Cumin Powder

1 tsp dried Oregano

½ cup heavy Whipping Cream

1 cup Sour Cream

Directions:

1. Select Sear/Sauté mode and set to Medium. Melt the butter, and add onion and chicken.

2. Stir and let cook the chicken for 6 minutes. Stir in the cannellini beans, cumin powder, oregano, salt, and pepper.

3. Pour in the broth, stir, close the pressure lid, and secure the pressure valve.Select Pressure mode on High for 10 minutes. Press Start/Stop.

4. Once the timer has ended, let the pot sit uncovered for 10 minutes, then do a quick pressure release. Stir in the whipping and sour cream.

5. Close the crisping lid and select Broil mode. Cook for 2 minutes.

6. Serve warm with a mix of steamed bell peppers and broccoli.

Nutrition facts Nutrition facts per serving:

Calories 535; Fat 33g; Sodium 340mg; Carbs 15g; Protein 46.7g

PORK

EXCITING PORK CHOPS WITH MUSHROOM GRAVY

Meant to be a simple gravy but the mushrooms give it more worth. This passes for something you can make for your special someone who will be excited to enjoy this dish.

Preparation Time: 5 minutes | Cooking Time: 30 minutes | Servings: 4

Ingredients:

4 Pork Chops

1 tbsp Olive Oil

3 cloves Garlic, minced

Salt and Pepper, to taste

1 tsp Garlic Powder

1 (10 oz) can Mushroom Soup

8 oz Cremini Mushrooms, sliced

1 small Onion, chopped

1 cup Beef Broth

1 sprig Fresh Thyme

Chopped Parsley to garnish

Directions:

1. Select Sear/Sauté mode. Add oil, mushrooms, garlic, and onion. Sauté them, stirring occasionally with a spoon, until nice and translucent, for 3 minutes.
2. Season the pork chops with salt, garlic powder, and pepper, and add them to the pot followed by the thyme and broth. Seal the lid and select Pressure mode on High pressure for 10 minutes. Press Start/Stop to start cooking.
3. Once the timer has ended, do a natural pressure release for about 10 minutes, then a quick pressure release to let the remaining steam out.
4. Close the crisping lid and cook on Broil mode for 5 minutes.
5. When ready, add the mushroom soup. Stir it until the mixture thickens a little bit. Dish the pork and gravy into a serving bowl and garnish with parsley.
6. Serve with a side of creamy sweet potato mash.

Nutrition facts Nutrition facts per serving:

Calories 423; Fat 18.5g; Sodium 560mg; Carbs 13g; Protein 35.5g

HONEY-MUSTARD PORK TENDERLOIN

It is amazing how this tenderloin cooks in very little time than expected and this should be the case when cooking meat to not kill the nutrients in the food. It is a combination of sweetness from the monk fruit sugar and sharpness from the vinegar, but in all, it is SUPER tasty.

Preparation Time: 10 minutes | Cooking Time: 20 minutes | Servings: 4

Ingredients:

2 lb Pork Tenderloin

2 tbsp Olive Oil

¼ cup Honey

½ cup Chicken Broth

Salt and Black Pepper to taste

1 clove Garlic, minced

1 tsp Sage Powder

1 tbsp Dijon Mustard

¼ cup Balsamic Vinegar

1 tbsp Worcestershire Sauce

½ tbsp Cornstarch

4 tbsp Water

Directions:

1. Put the pork on a clean flat surface and pat dry using paper towels. Season with salt and pepper. Select Sear/Sauté mode.
2. Heat the oil and brown the pork on both sides, for about 4 minutes in total. Remove the pork onto a plate and set aside.
3. Add in honey, chicken broth, balsamic vinegar, garlic, Worcestershire sauce, mustard, and sage. Stir the ingredients and return the pork to the pot.
4. Close the lid, secure the pressure valve, and select Pressure mode on High for 15 minutes. Once the timer has ended, do a quick pressure release.
5. Remove the pork with tongs onto a plate and wrap it in aluminum foil.
6. Next, mix the cornstarch with water and pour it into the pot. Select Sear/Sauté mode, stir the mixture and cook until it thickens. Then, turn the pot off after the desired thickness is achieved.
7. Unwrap the pork and use a knife to slice it with 3 to 4-inch thickness. Arrange the slices on a serving platter and spoon the sauce all over it.
8. Serve with a syrupy sautéed Brussels sprouts and red onion chunks.

Nutrition facts Nutrition facts per serving:

Calories 432; Fat 12.1g; Sodium 440mg; Carbs 21.2g; Protein 43.3g

PORK ROAST WITH HERB GRAVY

Tweak up a regular gravy with some coffee and be in awe at the aroma. I like the entire introduction of Italian seasoning and ranch dressing to this meat dish. It offers a different, off the usual kind of satisfaction.

Preparation Time: 5 minutes | Cooking Time: 20 minutes | Servings: 4

Ingredients:

2 lb Pork Roast, cut into 2-inch slabs

1 tbsp Italian Seasoning

1 tbsp Ranch Dressing

1 tsp Red Wine Vinegar

2 cloves Garlic, minced

Salt and Pepper, to taste

1 small Onion, chopped

1 tbsp Olive Oil

2 tsp Onion Powder

½ tsp Paprika

2 cups Beef Broth

2 tbsp Cornstarch

2 tbsp Water

Chopped parsley to garnish

Directions:

1. Season the pork roast with salt and pepper, and set aside.
2. In a bowl, add Italian seasoning, ranch dressing, red wine vinegar, garlic, onion powder, and paprika.
3. Open the pot, select Sear/Sauté mode, and heat the oil. Sauté the onion, until translucent. Pour the gravy mixture and broth over and add the pork.
4. Close the lid, secure the pressure valve, and select Pressure mode on High pressure for 15 minutes. Press Start/Stop to start cooking.
5. Once the timer has ended, do a quick pressure release, and open the pot.
6. Remove the pork roast with a slotted spoon onto a serving plate.
7. Mix the cornstarch with the water in a small bowl and add it to the sauce. Select Sear/Sauté. Stir and cook the sauce for 4 minutes, until thickens.
8. Once the gravy is ready, turn off the pot and spoon the sauce over the pork.
9. Garnish with parsley and serve with a turnip mash.

Nutrition facts Nutrition facts per serving:

Calories 483; Fat 15g; Sodium 590mg; Carbs 23g; Protein 49g

GINGER AND GARLIC PORK TENDERLOIN WITH SOY SAUCE

Ginger is one spice to always have in the kitchen when cooking an asian-style dish. It has incredible colon cleansing benefits that really aid you when you are losing weight. Combined with soy sauce in this pork dish, you can only expect a health pack into your system with pleasant aromas.

Preparation Time: 3 minutes | Cooking Time: 20 minutes | Servings: 4

Ingredients:

2 lb Pork Tenderloin

½ cup Soy Sauce

¼ cup Sugar

½ cup Water + 2 tbsp Water

3 tbsp grated Ginger

2 cloves Garlic, minced

2 tbsp Sesame Oil

2 tsp Cornstarch

Chopped Scallions to garnish

Sesame Seeds to garnish

Directions:

1. In the cooker's inner pot, add soy sauce, sugar, half cup of water, ginger, garlic, and sesame oil. Use a spoon to stir them. Then, add the pork.
2. Close the lid, secure the pressure valve, and select Pressure mode on High pressure for 12 minutes. Press Start/Stop.
3. Once the timer has ended, do a quick pressure release, and open the pot.
4. Remove the pork and set aside.
5. In a bowl, mix the cornstarch with the remaining water until smooth and pour it into the pot. Bring back the pork. Close the crisping lid and press Broil.
6. Cook for 5 minutes, until the sauce has thickened. Stir the sauce frequently, every 1-2 minutes, to avoid burning. Once the sauce is ready, serve the pork with a side endive salad or steamed veggies. Spoon the sauce all over it.

Nutrition facts Nutrition facts per serving:

Calories 478; Fat 19g; Sodium 1617mg; Carbs 13g; Protein 51g

QUICK PORK ROAST SANDWICH WITH SLAW

Got some pork roast in the fridge and trying to make something quick on a lazy day? This sandwich recipe is for you! Cook them into a pulled pork style, load your buns with it, and munch away with no shame.

Preparation Time: 5 minutes | Cooking Time: 15 minutes | Servings: 8

Ingredients:

2 lb Chuck Roast

¼ cup Sugar

1 tsp Spanish Paprika

1 tsp Garlic Powder

1 White Onion, sliced

2 cups Beef Broth

Salt to taste

2 tbsp Apple Cider Vinegar

Assembling:

4 Buns, halved

1 cup White Cheddar Cheese, grated

4 tbsp Mayonnaise

1 cup Red Cabbage, shredded

1 cup White Cabbage, shredded

Directions:

1. Place the pork roast on a clean flat surface and sprinkle with paprika, garlic powder, sugar, and salt. Use your hands to rub the seasoning on the meat.
2. Open the cooker, add beef broth, onions, pork, and apple cider vinegar.
3. Close the lid, secure the pressure valve, and select Pressure mode on High pressure for 12 minutes. Press Start/Stop.
4. Once the timer has ended, do a quick pressure release. Remove the roast to a cutting board, and use two forks to shred them. Return to the pot, close the crisping lid, and cook for 3 minutes on Air Crisp at 300 F.
5. In the buns, spread the mayo, add the shredded pork, some cooked onions from the pot, and shredded red and white cabbage. Top with the cheese.

Nutrition facts Nutrition facts per serving:

Calories 387; Fat 21g; Sodium 450mg; Carbs 21.3g; Protein 27g

TERRIFIC HOMEMADE BBQ RIBS

A must do with your Multicooker. You don't need a grill to enjoy a barbecue anymore. Right here, is an amazing option to make and guess what, your guests will be all finger licking when they have it.

Preparation Time: 7 minutes | Cooking Time: 35 minutes | Servings: 2

Ingredients:

½ lb rack Baby Back Ribs

Salt and Pepper to season

¼ cup Beef Broth

½ cup Barbecue Sauce

3 tbsp Apple Cider Vinegar

Directions:

1. Select Sear/Sauté mode. Heat the oil into the pot. Meanwhile, season the ribs with salt and pepper. Cook them to brown, for 1 to 2 minutes per side.
2. Pour the barbecue sauce, broth, and apple cider vinegar over the ribs and use tongs to flip so they are well coated.
3. Close the lid and pressure valve and set to Pressure mode on High pressure for 30 minutes. Press Start/Stop to start cooking.
4. Once the timer goes off, do a natural pressure release for 12 minutes, then a quick pressure release to let out the remaining steam.
5. Close the crisping lid and set to Air Crisp mode for 5 minutes at 350 F. Make sure the sauce is thick enough.
6. Use a knife to slice the ribs and over the sauce all over it.
7. Serve the ribs with a generous side of steamed but crunchy green beans.

Nutrition facts Nutrition facts per serving:

Calories 387; Fat 17g; Sodium 670mg; Carbs 31g; Protein 24g

HEAVENLY BANGERS WITH MASHED POTATOES & ONION GRAVY

Bangers and mash are on my top list of convenient foods while offering the body with so many nutrients. Here's the tastiest recipe to find, make sure to make more for others too. It is that good!

Preparation Time: 5 minutes | Cooking Time: 35 minutes | Servings: 4

Ingredients:

2 lb Potatoes, peeled and halved

4 Italian Sausages

1 cup Water + 2 tbsp Water

⅓ cup Green Onion, sliced

Salt and Pepper, to taste

4 tbsp Milk

¼ cup + 2 tbsp + 2 tbsp Butter

1 tbsp Cornstarch

3 tbsp Balsamic Vinegar

1 Onion, sliced thinly

1 cup + 2 tbsp Beef Broth

Directions:

1. Put the potatoes in the inner pot and pour the water over. Seal the lid; select Steam mode on High for 15 minutes and press Start/Stop.

2. Do a quick pressure release, and remove the potatoes to a bowl. Add in a quarter cup butter and use a masher to mash them until the butter is well mixed. Slowly add the milk and mix it using a spoon. Add the green onions, season with pepper and salt and fold it in with the spoon. Set aside. Pour out the liquid in the cooker, and use paper towels to wipe inside the pot dry. Select Sear/Sauté mode and melt two tablespoons of butter.

3. Brown the sausages on each side for 3 minutes. Remove to the potato mash and cover with aluminium foil to keep warm. Set aside Back into the pot, add the two tablespoons of the beef broth to deglaze the bottom of the pot while stirring and scraping the bottom with a spoon. Add the remaining butter and onions; sauté the onions until translucent, then pour in the balsamic vinegar. Stir for another minute.

4. In a bowl, mix the cornstarch with water and pour into the pot. Add the remaining beef broth. Allow the sauce to thicken and adjust the seasoning. Turn off the heat once a slurry is formed. Dish the mashed potatoes and sausages in serving plates. Spoon the gravy over it and serve immediately with steamed green beans.

Nutrition facts Nutrition facts per serving:

Calories 567; Fat 36g; Sodium 670mg; Carbs 45g; Protein 22g

BRAISED PORK NECK BONES

I will recommend having this dish on the menu for a family get-together dinner. A little drizzle on steamed veggies is amazing. Then, with a broccoli mash, words can't explain the taste, and with rice, girl, you'll be up for a fantastic time.

Preparation Time: 4 minutes | Cooking Time: 35 minutes | Servings: 6

Ingredients:

3 lb Pork Neck Bones

4 tbsp Olive Oil

Salt and Black Pepper to taste

2 cloves Garlic, smashed

1 tbsp Tomato Paste

1 tsp dried Thyme

1 White Onion, sliced

½ cup Red Wine

1 cup Beef Broth

Directions:

1. Open the lid and select Sear/Sauté mode. Warm the olive oil.
2. Meanwhile, season the pork neck bones with salt and pepper. After, place them in the oil to brown on all sides. Work in batches.
3. Each batch should cook in about 5 minutes. Then, remove them onto a plate.
4. Add the onion and season with salt to taste. Stir with a spoon and cook the onions until soft, for a few minutes.
5. Then, add garlic, thyme, pepper, and tomato paste. Cook them for 2 minutes, constant stirring to prevent the tomato paste from burning.
6. Next, pour the red wine into the pot to deglaze the bottom. Add the pork neck bones back to the pot and pour the beef broth over it.
7. Close the lid, secure the pressure valve, and select Pressure mode on High pressure for 10 minutes. Press Start/Stop to start cooking.
8. Once the timer has ended, let the pot sit for 10 minutes before doing a quick pressure release. Close the crisping lid and cook on Broil mode for 5 minutes, until nice and tender.
9. Dish the pork neck into a serving bowl and serve with the red wine sauce spooned over and a right amount of broccoli mash.

Nutrition facts Nutrition facts per serving:

Calories 487; Fat 36.5g; Sodium 329mg; Carbs 5g; Protein 33.4g

MUSTARDY PORK LOIN WITH VEGETABLE SAUCE

A bit of protein, a bit of good fat, and a bit of vitamins is what you have right here in this recipe. You can make some more steamed veggies to enjoy the sauce with or have it with a side of steamed green.

Preparation Time: 7 minutes | Cooking Time: 28 minutes | Servings: 4

Ingredients:

2 lb Pork Loin Roast

Salt and Pepper, to taste

3 cloves Garlic, minced

1 medium Onion, diced

2 tbsp Butter

3 stalks Celery, chopped

3 Carrots, chopped

1 cup Chicken Broth

2 tbsp Worcestershire Sauce

½ tbsp Sugar

1 tsp Yellow Mustard

2 tsp dried Basil

2 tsp dried Thyme

1 tbsp Cornstarch

¼ cup Water

Directions:

1. Select Sear/Sauté mode, and heat oil. Season the pork with salt and pepper. Sear the pork to golden brown on both sides.

2. Then, add the garlic and onions, and cook them until soft, for about 4 minutes. Top with the celery, carrots, chicken broth, Worcestershire sauce, mustard, thyme, basil, and sugar.

3. Close the lid, secure the pressure valve, and select Pressure mode on High pressure for 15 minutes. Press Start/Stop to start cooking.

4. Once the timer is off, do a quick pressure release. Next, add the cornstarch to the water, in a bowl, and mix with a spoon, until nice and smooth.

5. Add it to the pot, close the crisping lid, and cook on Broil mode, for 3 - 5 minutes, until the sauce becomes a slurry with a bit of thickness, and the pork is nice and tender.

6. Adjust the seasoning, and ladle to a serving platter. Serve with a side of steamed almond garlicky rapini mix.

Nutrition facts Nutrition facts per serving:

Calories 543; Fat 26.1g; Sodium 360mg; Carbs 16g; Protein 55.7g

PORK ROAST WITH SPICY PEANUT SAUCE

Peanuts are well-embraced ingredients in the American cuisine, and the combination with pork here brings a new kind of aroma that you will just love. Try it now and always!

Preparation Time: 8 minutes | Cooking Time: 20 minutes | Servings: 6

Ingredients:

3 lb Pork Roast

1 cup Hot Water

1 large Red Bell Pepper, seeded and sliced

Salt and Pepper to taste

1 large White Onion, sliced

½ cup Soy Sauce

1 tbsp Plain Vinegar

½ cup Peanut Butter

1 tbsp Lime Juice

1 tbsp Garlic Powder

1 tsp Ginger Puree

2 Chilies, deseeded, chopped

To Garnish:

Chopped Peanuts

Chopped Green Onions

Lime Wedges

Directions:

1. Add the soy sauce, vinegar, peanut butter, lime juice, garlic powder, chilies, and ginger puree, to a bowl. Whisk together and even. Add a few pinches of salt and pepper, and mix it.
2. Open the cooker lid, and place the pork in the inner pot. Pour the hot water and peanut butter mixture over it.
3. Close the lid, secure the pressure valve, and select Pressure mode on High pressure for 15 minutes. Press Start/Stop to start cooking.
4. Once the timer has stopped, do a quick pressure release.
5. Use two forks to shred it, inside the pot, and close the crisping lid.
6. Cook on Broil mode for 4 - 5 minutes, until the sauce thickens.
7. On a bed of cooked rice, spoon the meat with some sauce and garnish it with the chopped peanuts, green onions, and the lemon wedges.

Nutrition facts Nutrition facts per serving:

Calories 591; Fat 26.6g; Sodium 330mg; Carbs 20g; Protein 57g

GREEK TENDER PORK ROAST

Yup! Something that doesn't take a struggle of the teeth to enjoy. This recipe takes a while with the good aim of tenderizing the pork so that it can be easily eating in a salad or a sandwich; or better still refrigerated and used in a stew. You will need about one hour for this but worth the time.

Preparation Time: 4 minutes | Cooking Time: 55 minutes | Servings: 6

Ingredients:

3 lb Pork Roast, cut into 3-inch pieces

3 tbsp Cavender's Greek Seasoning to taste

1 tsp Onion Powder

1 cup Beef Broth

½ cup Kalamata Olives, pitted

¼ cup fresh Lemon Juice

Salt to taste

Directions:

1. Put the pork chunks in the inner pot of the cooker.
2. In a bowl, add greek seasoning, onion powder, beef broth, lemon juice, olives, and salt to taste. Mix using a spoon and pour the sauce over the pork.
3. Close the lid, secure the pressure valve, and select Pressure mode on High pressure for 35 minutes. Press Start/Stop to start cooking.
4. Once the timer is off, do a natural pressure release for 10 minutes, then do a quick pressure release to let out any more steam, and open the pot.
5. Use two forks to shred the roast inside to pot and close the crisping lid. Cook on Broil mode for 10 minutes, until nice and tender.
6. Serve with a green salad, potatoes or rice.

Nutrition facts Nutrition facts per serving:

Calories 478; Fat 22.41g; Sodium 288mg; Carbs 5g; Protein 52.95g

GINGERY PORK WITH COCONUT SAUCE

The coconut and ginger in this dish bring out this exotic flavor, almost reminding you or making you dream of a beach? Vacation somewhere on the Indian Ocean. Well, don't dream too far, right there on your dining table, this dish creates that experience.

Preparation Time: 4 minutes | Cooking Time: 40 minutes | Servings: 6

Ingredients:

3 lb Shoulder Roast

1 tbsp Olive Oil

Salt and Black Pepper to season

2 cups Coconut Milk

1 tsp Coriander Powder

1 tsp Cumin Powder

3 tbsp grated Ginger

3 tsp minced Garlic

½ cup Beef Broth

1 Onion, peeled and quartered

Parsley Leaves (unchopped), to garnish

Directions:

1. In a bowl, add coriander, salt, pepper, and cumin. Use a spoon to mix them.

2. Season the pork with the spice mixture. Rub the spice onto meat, with hands.

3. Open the lid of cooker, add olive oil, pork, onions, ginger, garlic, broth and coconut milk.

4. Close the lid, secure the pressure valve, and select Pressure mode on High for 30 minutes. Press Start/Stop to start cooking.

5. Once the timer has stopped, do a quick pressure release. Give it a good stir and close the crisping lid. Cook for 10 minutes on Broil mode, until you perfect texture and creaminess.

6. Dish the meat with the sauce into a serving bowl, garnish it with the parsley and serve with a side of bread or cooked shrimp.

Nutrition facts Nutrition facts per serving:

Calories 491; Fat 31g; Sodium 237mg; Carbs 13g; Protein 38g

SPICED PORK CARNITAS IN LETTUCE CUPS

Can't have a high carb burger, lettuce leaves are here to save. Make this flavorful pulled pork recipe and assemble them with grated carrots in the lettuce leaves. It is that simple to enjoy.

Prep Time: 9 min | Cooking Time: 20 min + overnight refrigerated | Servings: 6

Ingredients:

3 lb Pork Shoulder

2 tbsp Olive Oil

1 small head Butter Lettuce, leaves removed, washed and dried

2 Limes, cut in wedges

2 Carrots, grated

1 ½ cup Water

1 Onion, chopped

½ tsp Cayenne Pepper

½ tsp Coriander Powder

1 tsp Cumin Powder

1 tsp Garlic Powder

1 tsp White Pepper

2 tsp dried Oregano

1 tsp Red Pepper Flakes

Salt to taste

Directions:

1. In a bowl, add onion, cayenne, coriander, garlic, cumin, white pepper, dried oregano, red pepper flakes, and salt. Mix them well with a spoon.
2. Drizzle over the pork and rub to coat. Then, wrap the meat in plastic wrap and refrigerate overnight.
3. On the next day, open the cooker lid, and select Sear/Sauté mode.
4. Pour 2 tablespoons of olive oil in the pot and while heating, take the pork out from the fridge, remove the wraps and place it in the pot.
5. Brown it on both sides for 6 minutes and then pour the water.
6. Close the lid, secure the pressure valve, and select Pressure mode on High pressure for 15 minutes. Press Start/Stop to start cooking.
7. Once the timer has stopped, do a quick pressure release.Use two forks to shred the pork, inside the pot. Close the crisping lid, and select Bake/Roast mode. Set for 10 minutes at 350 F. When ready, turn off the heat and begin assembling.
8. Arrange double layers of lettuce leaves on a flat surface, make a bed of grated carrots in them, and spoon the pulled pork on them.
9. Drizzle a sauce of choice (I used mustardy sauce) over them, and serve with lime wedges for freshness.

Nutrition facts Nutrition facts per serving:

Calories 612; Fat 38.6g; Sodium 521mg; Carbs 10g; Protein 58.27g

PORK AND SWEET POTATO CHILI

Massive aromas gush out of this dish. I like the greeny effect it has which communicates HEALTHY. I prefer to have this chili with chips or crusted bread because the satisfaction is pleasant, but you can have it with some steamed root veggies. Remember, moderation though!

Preparation Time: 5 minutes | Cooking Time: 65 minutes | Servings: 6

Ingredients:

1 ½ lb Pork Roast, cut into 1-inch cubes

1 lb Tomatillos, husks removed

2 tbsp Olive Oil, divided into 2

1 bulb Garlic, tail sliced off, peeled

2 Green Chilies

3 cups Chicken Broth

1 Green Bell Pepper, seeded and chopped

Salt and Pepper, to taste

½ tsp Cumin Powder

1 tsp dried Oregano

1 Bay Leaf

1 bunch Cilantro, chopped

2 Sweet Potatoes, cut into ½-inch cubes

Directions:

1. Put the garlic bulb in a baking dish that fits in your reversible rack, inside the inner pot. Drizzle a bit of 1 portion of olive oil over the garlic bulb.

2. Place the green bell peppers, onion, green chilies, and tomatillos on the dish in a single layer.

3. Close the crisping lid and cook for 15 minutes at 400 F on Air Crisp mode.

4. Then, remove them, and set aside to cool. Wipe clean the pot if needed.

5. Place the garlic in a blender. Add green bell pepper, tomatillos, onions, and green chilies. Pulse for a few minutes not to be smooth but slightly chunky.

6. Now, open the lid of the cooker, and select Sear/Sauté mode.

7. Pour in the remaining olive oil and while is heating, season the pork cubes with salt and pepper. Then, brown the pork, for about 5 minutes.

8. Stir in oregano, cumin, bay leaf, pour in the blended green sauce, potatoes, and add the chicken broth. Stir well.

9. Close the lid, secure the pressure valve, and select Pressure mode on High pressure for 25 minutes. Press Start/Stop to start cooking.

10. Once the timer has ended, let the pot sit closed for 10 minutes.

11. After, do a natural pressure release for 5 minutes, and then a quick pressure release to let the remaining steam out.

12. Open the pot. Remove and discard the bay leaf, add half of the cilantro, adjust with salt and pepper, and stir.
13. Close the crisping lid to give it nice and tender taste. Cook on Broil mode for 10 minutes.
14. Dish the chili into serving bowls and garnish it with the remaining chopped cilantro.
15. Serve topped with a side of chips or crusted bread.

Nutrition facts Nutrition facts per serving:

Calories 410; Fat 18g; Sodium 90mg; Carbs 16g; Protein 37g

SAVORY HAM WITH COLLARD GREENS

Really simple recipe, but filled with a lot of good nutrients. It cooks in no time, so you needn't worry when you get trapped in hunger. Put everything together in the pot, hit start, and get your plate ready.

Preparation Time: 4 minutes | Cooking Time: 5 minutes | Servings: 4

Ingredients:

20 oz Collard Greens, washed and cut

2 cubes of Chicken Bouillon

4 cups Water

½ cup diced Sweet Onion

2 ½ cups diced Ham

Directions:

1. Place the ham at the bottom of the inner pot. Add collard greens and onion.
2. Then, add chicken cubes to the water and dissolve it.
3. Pour the mixture into the pot. Close the lid, secure the pressure valve, to seal properly.
4. Select Steam mode on High pressure for 5 minutes. Press Start/Stop.
5. Once the timer has ended, do a quick pressure release, and open the lid.
6. Spoon the vegetables and the ham with sauce into a serving platter.
7. Serve with a side of steak dish of your choice.

Nutrition facts Nutrition facts per serving:

Calories 178; Fat 3.5g; Sodium 527mg; Carbs 10g; Protein 26.5g

CREAMY RANCH PORK CHOPS

Just five ingredients giving you creamy goodness, what else can you wish for? Put all the ingredients in the Multicooker, hit Start, and rush to get a quick shower. On return, the dish will be near done to fill up your hungry tummy.

Preparation Time: 2 minutes | Cooking Time: 20 minutes | Servings: 4

Ingredients:

4 Pork Loin Chops

1 (15 oz) can Mushroom Soup Cream

1 oz Ranch Dressing and Seasoning Mix

½ cup Chicken Broth

Chopped Parsley to garnish

Directions:

1. Add pork, mushroom soup cream, ranch dressing and seasoning mix, and chicken broth, inside the inner pot of your cooker.
2. Close the lid, secure the pressure valve, and select Pressure mode on High pressure for 10 minutes. Press Start/Stop.
3. Once the timer has ended, do a natural pressure release for 10 minutes, then a quick pressure release to let the remaining steam out.
4. Close the crisping lid and cook for 5 minutes on Broil mode, until tender.
5. Serve with well-seasoned sautéed cremini mushrooms, and the sauce.

Nutrition facts Nutrition facts per serving:

Calories 463; Fat 18.9g; Sodium 381mg; Carbs 14g; Protein 39.1g

BEEF

JUICY BEEF & BROCCOLI

One of the very first things you should make if you're in your early days of using your new Multicooker. Beef and broccoli are a long existing recipe but the taste and nutrients derived never disappoint. So, you definitely should make it now and even often.

Preparation Time: 5 minutes | Cooking Time: 30 minutes | Servings: 4

Ingredients:

2 lb Chuck Roast, boneless and cut into thin strips

4 cloves Garlic, minced

7 cups Broccoli Florets

1 tbsp Olive Oil

1 cup Beef Broth

1 tbsp Cornstarch

¾ cup Soy Sauce

Salt to taste

Directions:

1. Open the lid of cooker, and select Sear/Sauté mode.
2. Add the olive oil, and once heated, add the beef and minced garlic. Cook the meat until brown. Stir in soy sauce and beef broth.
3. Close the lid, secure the pressure valve, and select Pressure mode on High pressure for 10 minutes. Press Start/Stop to start cooking.
4. Once the timer has ended, do a quick pressure release and remove the meat and set aside. Use a soup spoon to fetch out a quarter of the liquid into a bowl, add the cornstarch, and mix it until it is well dissolved.
5. Pour the starch mixture into the pot and place the reversible rack. Place the broccoli florets on it and seal the pressure lid. Select Steam mode on LOW for 5 minutes.
6. When ready, do a quick pressure release and open the lid. Remove the rack, stir the sauce, add the meat and close the crisping lid.
7. Cook for 5 minutes on Broil mode. The sauce should be thick enough when you finish cooking. Dish the beef broccoli sauce into a serving bowl and serve with a side of cooked pasta.

Nutrition facts Nutrition facts per serving:

Calories 355; Fat 12.8g; Sodium 506mg; Carbs 9g; Protein 41.8g

RUSSIAN BEEFY UNSTUFFED CABBAGE STEW

Very ideal for lunch, this sauce is heavy. A bit over a bed of pumpkin mash goes a long way to nourish your body. Kids may be picky on this one because of the big chunks of cabbage so make the vegetables in smaller cuts when there are kids.

Preparation Time: 8 minutes | Cooking Time: 21 minutes | Servings: 4

Ingredients:

1 cup Rice

1 large head Cabbage, cut in chunks

1 lb Ground Beef

Salt and Black Pepper to taste

½ cup chopped Onion

4 cloves Garlic, minced

2 tbsp Butter

1 Bay Leaf

1 cup diced Tomatoes

1 ½ cup Beef Broth

¼ cup Plain Vinegar

2 tbsp Worcestershire Sauce

1 tbsp Paprika Powder

1 tbsp dried Oregano

Chopped parsley to garnish

Directions:

1. Set the cooker on Sear/Sauté mode. Melt the butter and add the beef.
2. Brown it for about 6 minutes and add in the onions, garlic, and bay leaf. Stir and cook for 2 more minutes.
3. Stir in the oregano, paprika, salt, pepper, rice, cabbage, vinegar, broth, and Worcestershire sauce. Cook for 3 minutes, stirring occassionally.
4. Add the tomatoes but don't stir. Close the lid, secure the pressure valve, and select Pressure Cook mode on High for 5 minutes. Press Start/Stop.
5. Once the timer is done, let the pot sit closed for 5 minutes and then do a quick pressure. Open the lid.
6. Stir the sauce, remove the bay leaf, and adjust the seasoning with salt.
7. Dish the cabbage sauce in serving bowls and serve with bread rolls.

Nutrition facts Nutrition facts per serving:

Calories 521; Fat 15.31g; Sodium 369mg; Carbs 44.97g; Protein 38.81g

HOAGIE BEEF BURGERS WITH PROVOLONE CHEESE

A great option to have for lunch using hoagies to certify your safety. It takes quite a while to make, but each bite is smooth because the meat has been tenderized for easy bites. Have fun making it with your choice of cheese, I used Provolone Cheese here, but you can try with any other.

Preparation Time: 5 minutes | Cooking Time: 60 minutes | Servings: 4

Ingredients:

1 tbsp Olive Oil

1 (14 oz) can French Onion Soup

1 lb Chuck Beef Roast

1 Onion, sliced

2 tbsp Worcestershire Sauce

2 Cups Beef Broth

Salt and Black Pepper to taste

1 tsp Garlic Powder

3 Slices Provolone Cheese

3 Hoagies, halved

3 tsp Mayonnaise

Directions:

1. Season the beef with garlic powder, salt, and pepper.
2. On cooker, select Sear/Sauté mode. Heat the olive oil and brown the beef on both sides for about 5 minutes. Remove the meat onto a plate.
3. Into the pot, add the onions and cook until soft. Then, pour the beef broth and stir, while scraping the bottom off every stuck bit. Add the onion soup, Worcestershire sauce, and beef.
4. Close the lid, secure the pressure valve, and select Pressure mode on High pressure for 20 minutes. Press Start/Stop.
5. Once the timer has stopped, do a natural pressure release for 10-15 minutes, and then a quick pressure release to let out any remaining steam.
6. Use two forks to shred the meat. Close the crisping lid and cook on Bake/Roast for 10 minutes at 350 F.
7. When ready, open the lid and strain the juice of the pot through a sieve into a bowl to be used as "Au Jus" for serving.
8. Assemble the burgers by slathering mayo on halved hoagies, spoon the shredded meat over and top each hoagie with cheese. Serve with the "Au Jus" as a dip.

Nutrition facts Nutrition facts per serving:

Calories 435; Fat 23.2g; Sodium 410mg; Carbs 9.3g; Protein 36.3g

TRICOLOR PEPPER ROLLED BEEF WITH ONION GRAVY

I'm one for aromas, and this beef dish exudes so much of it. Make it for lunch, for dinner or a festive celebration, and you'll be all cheers for putting in the effort.

Preparation Time: 20 minutes | Cooking Time: 42 minutes | Servings: 6

Ingredients:

2 lb Round Steak Pieces, about 6 to 8 pieces

½ Green Bell Pepper, finely chopped

½ Red Bell Pepper, finely chopped

½ Yellow Bell Pepper, finely chopped

1 Yellow Onion, finely chopped

2 cloves Garlic, minced

Salt and Pepper, to taste

¼ cup All-purpose Flour

2 tbsp Olive Oil

½ cup Water

Directions:

1. Wrap the steaks in plastic wrap, place on a cutting board, and use a rolling pin to pound flat of about 2-inch thickness.
2. Remove the plastic wrap and season them with salt and pepper. Set aside.
3. Put the chopped peppers, onion, and garlic in a bowl, and mix them evenly.
4. Spoon the bell pepper mixture onto the flattened steaks and roll them to have the peppers inside.
5. Use some toothpicks to secure the beef rolls and dredge the steaks in all-purpose flour while shaking off any excess flour. Place them in a plate.
6. Select Sear/Sauté mode on cooker and heat the oil. Add the beef rolls and brown them on both sides, for about 6 minutes.
7. Pour the water over the meat, close the lid, secure the pressure valve, and select Pressure mode on High pressure for 20 minutes. Press Start/Stop.
8. Once the timer has stopped, do a natural pressure release for 10 minutes. Close the crisping lid and cook for 10 minutes on Broil mode.
9. When ready, Remove the meat to a plate and spoon the sauce from the pot over. Serve the stuffed meat rolls with a side of steamed veggies.

Nutrition facts Nutrition facts per serving:

Calories 396; Fat 21.5g; Sodium 540mg; Carbs 7g; Protein 46g

HEALTHY BEEF TACO SOUP

Sounds great to have tacos night? You definitely can in soup and guess what? It tastes better. The ingredients used in this recipe are nutrient packed which are good to keep you in check on your weight loss program.

Preparation Time: 10 minutes | Cooking Time: 20 minutes | Servings: 8

Ingredients:

2 tbsp Olive Oil

6 Green Bell pepper, diced

2 medium Yellow Onion, chopped

3 lb Ground Beef, grass fed

Salt and Black Pepper to taste

3 tbsp Chili Powder

2 tbsp Cumin Powder

2 tsp Paprika

1 tsp Garlic Powder

1 tsp Cinnamon

1 tsp Onion Powder

6 cups chopped Tomatoes

½ cup chopped Green Chilies

3 cups Bone Broth

3 cups Milk

Topping:

Chopped Jalapenos, Cilantro and Green   Onions, Sliced Avocados, Lime Juice

Directions:

1. Select Sear/Sauté mode and set High on your cooker. Pour in the oil, once it has heated, add the yellow onion and green peppers.
2. Sauté until they are soft for about 5 minutes. Include the ground beef, stir the ingredients, and let the beef cook for about 8 minutes until it browns.
3. Next, add the chili powder, cumin powder, black pepper, paprika, cinnamon, garlic powder, onion powder, and green chilies. Give them a good stir.
4. Top with tomatoes, milk, and bone broth. Close the lid, secure the pressure valve, and select Pressure mode on High for 20 minutes. Press Start.
5. Once the timer has ended, do a quick pressure release. Adjust the taste with salt and pepper. Dish the taco soup into serving bowls and add the toppings.
6. Serve warm with a side of tortillas.

Nutrition facts Nutrition facts per serving:

Calories 522; Fat 25.3g; Sodium 289mg; Carbs 21g; Protein 48.5g

ASIAN-STYLE RED BEEF CURRY

This sauce is in a class of its own flavors and slightly different from the normal you often have. It gets ready in 30 minutes so you can plan to make it ahead before the hunger pangs set in.

Preparation Time: 5 minutes | Cooking Time: 33 minutes | Servings: 4

Ingredients:

1 ½ lb Beef Brisket, cut in cubes

1 tbsp Olive Oil

2 cloves Garlic, minced

¼-inch Ginger, peeled and sliced

2 Bay Leaves

2 Star Anises

1 large Carrot, chopped

1 medium Onion, chopped

2 tbsp Red Curry Paste

1 cup Milk

1 Potato, peeled and chopped

1 tbsp Sugar

2 tsp Oyster Sauce

2 tsp Flour

3 tbsp Water

Directions:

1. Select Sear/Sauté mode. Heat oil, add garlic, ginger, and red curry paste.
2. Stir-fry them for 1 minute. Stir in onion and beef. Cook for 4 minutes.
3. Add the carrots, bay leaves, potato, star anises, sugar, and water. Stir.
4. Close the lid, secure the pressure valve, and select Pressure mode on High for 25 minutes. Press Start/Stop to start cooking.
5. Once the timer goes off, do a quick pressure release.
6. In a bowl, add the flour and 4 tablespoons of milk. Mix well with a spoon and pour it in the pot along with the oyster sauce and remaining milk. Stir it gently not to break the potato.
7. Close the crisping lid and cook on Broil mode for about 3 minutes, until the sauce thickens and meat is tender. After, turn off the pot.
8. Spoon the sauce into soup bowls and serve with a side of rice.

Nutrition facts Nutrition facts per serving:

Calories 434; Fat 25.6g; Sodium 545mg; Carbs 24g; Protein 27.6g

DELICIOUS PEPPER BEEF MIX

Anyone up for easy stir fry? There isn't the need to work up a stove top cooker to make this one. The Multicooker gets it all done with peppers that are super crunchy.

Preparation Time: 5 minutes | Cooking Time: 48 minutes | Servings: 4

Ingredients:

2 lb Beef Chuck Roast

1 tbsp Onion Powder

1 tbsp Garlic Powder

1 tbsp Italian Seasoning

Salt and Black Pepper to taste, cut in 4 pieces

1 cup Beef Broth

1 medium White Onion, sliced

1 Green Bell Pepper, seeded and sliced

1 Red Bell Pepper, seeded and sliced

2 tbsp Olive Oil

Directions:

1. Rub the beef with pepper, salt, garlic powder, Italian seasoning, and onion powder. Select Sear/Sauté mode on cooker.
2. Heat 1 tbsp oil, add the beef pieces and sear them on both sides until brown, for about 5 minutes. Use a pair of tongs to remove them onto a plate after. (You can do this in 2 batches).
3. Pour the beef broth and fish sauce into the pot to deglaze the bottom while you use a spoon to scrape any stuck beef bit at the bottom.
4. Add the meat back to the pot, close the lid, secure the pressure valve, and select Pressure mode on High pressure for 30 minutes. Press Start/Stop.
5. Once the timer has stopped, do a quick pressure release, and open the pot.
6. Use two forks to shred the beef, inside the pot. Close the crisping lid and select Broil mode for 10 minutes. When ready, set aside the meat and discard the liquid. Wipe clean the pot.
7. Select Sear/Sauté mode, heat the remaining oil, add the beef with onions and peppers. Sauté them for 3 minutes and season with salt and pepper.
8. Turn off the pot and dish the stir-fried beef into serving plates. Serve as a side to rice with sauce dish.

Nutrition facts Nutrition facts per serving:

Calories 487; Fat 21.7g; Sodium 370mg; Carbs 10g; Protein 54g

TRADITIONALLY-MADE BEEF BOURGUIGNONNE

Don't worry if you don't drink. Some types of alcohol contain 0 making them perfect to use for cooking. Right here this beef burgundy (bourguignonne) sauce proves it all.

Preparation Time: 10 minutes | Cooking Time: 33 minutes | Servings: 4

Ingredients:

2 lb Stewing Beef, cut in large chunks

Salt and Pepper, to taste

2 ½ tbsp Olive Oil

¼ tsp Red Wine Vinegar

¼ cup Pearl Onion

3 tsp Tomato Paste

½ lb Mushrooms, sliced

2 Carrots, peeled and chopped

1 Onion, sliced

2 cloves Garlic, crushed

1 cup Red Wine

2 cups Beef Broth

1 bunch Thyme

½ cup Cognac

2 tbsp All-purpose Flour

Directions:

1. Select Sear/Sauté mode. Season the beef with salt, pepper, and a light sprinkle of flour. Heat the oil in the pot, and brown the meat on all sides.

2. Pour the cognac into the pot and stir the mixture with a spoon to deglaze the bottom. Stir in thyme, red wine, broth, paste, garlic, mushrooms, onion, and pearl onions.

3. Close the lid, secure the pressure valve, and select Pressure mode on High for 25 minutes. Press Start/Stop.

4. Once the timer is off, do a natural pressure release for 10 minutes, then a quick pressure release to let out the remaining steam. Close the crisping lid and cook for 10 minutes on Broil mode. When ready, open the lid.

5. Use the spoon to remove the thyme, adjust the taste with salt and pepper, and add the vinegar. Stir the sauce and serve hot, with a side of rice.

Nutrition facts Nutrition facts per serving:

Calories 487; Fat 15.7g; Sodium 224mg; Carbs 14.2g; Protein 46.3g

5-MINUTE STEAK AND CHEESY STUFFED MUSHROOMS

Stuffed mushrooms are perfect when you want something light and easy for lunch, dinner, or even for brunch. What's exciting, you can use some leftover meat for it, and the cooker will turn it into something incredible.

Preparation Time: 5 minutes | Cooking Time: 5 minutes | Servings: 3

Ingredients:

6 large White Mushrooms, stems removed

2 cups cooked Leftover Beef, cut in very small cubes

2 tsp Garlic Salt

½ cup Vegetable Broth

2 oz Cream Cheese, softened

1 cup shredded Cheddar Cheese

1 tsp Olive Oil

Directions:

1. In a bowl, add the beef, garlic salt, cream cheese, and cheddar cheese. Use a spoon to mix them.
2. Spoon the beef mixture into the mushrooms and place the mushrooms in the inner pot of cooker. Drizzle them with olive oil, and add the broth.
3. Close the lid, secure the pressure valve, and select Pressure mode on High pressure for 3 minutes. Press Start/Stop to start cooking.
4. Once the timer is off, do a quick pressure release and open the pressure lid, discard the liquid, and remove the mushrooms.
5. Place the reversible rack and lay the mushrooms on it. Close the crisping lid and cook for 2 to 3 minutes on Air Crisp mode at 350 F.
6. Remove the stuffed mushrooms onto a plate, and serve hot with a side of steamed green veggies.

Nutrition facts Nutrition facts per serving:

Calories 315; Fat 17.5g; Sodium 142mg; Carbs 4g; Protein 24.3g

SAVORY CLASSIC POT ROAST

With an ultimate dish like this on the table, you needn't yell to get everyone around. It smells so good and tastes fantastic. Make a good choice of beef, trim off any excess fat with a knife, and head up to begin cooking.

Preparation Time: 4 minutes | Cooking Time: 30 minutes | Servings: 4

Ingredients:

2 lb Beef Chuck Roast

3 tbsp Olive Oil, divided into 2

Salt to taste

1 cup Beef Broth

1 packet Onion Soup Mix

1 cup chopped Broccoli

2 Red Bell Peppers, seeded and quartered

1 Yellow Onion, quartered

Directions:

1. Season the chuck roast with salt and set aside. Select Sear/Sauté mode on the cooker cooker.
2. Add the olive oil, and once heated, add the chuck roast. Sear for 5 minutes on each side. Then, pour in the beef broth.
3. In a zipper bag, add broccoli, onions, peppers, the remaining olive oil, and onion soup.
4. Close the bag and shake the mixture to coat the vegetables well. Use tongs to remove the vegetables into the pot and stir with a spoon.
5. Close the lid, secure the pressure valve, and select Pressure mode on High pressure for 18 minutes. Press Start/Stop.
6. Once the timer has stopped, do a quick pressure release, and open the pressure lid. Make cuts on the meat inside the pot and close the crisping lid.
7. Cook on Air Crisp mode for about 10 minutes, at 380 F, until nice and crispy.
8. Plate and serve with the vegetables and a drizzle of the sauce in the pot.

Nutrition facts Nutrition facts per serving:

Calories 492; Fat 23.8g; Sodium 347mg; Carbs 9g; Protein 55.2g

SAVORY BEER BEEF STEW

Another way to tweak things around if you are not up for wines. Find a beer and use it for this dish. Trust me, the aromas and tastes differ, and you will be glad that you tried it.

Preparation Time: 10 minutes | Cooking Time: 50 minutes | Servings: 4

Ingredients:

2 lb Beef Stewed Meat, cut into pieces

Salt and Black Pepper to taste

¼ cup All-purpose Flour

3 tbsp Butter

2 tbsp Worcestershire Sauce

2 cloves Garlic, minced

1 packet Dry Onion Soup Mix

2 cups Beef Broth

1 medium bottle Beer

1 tbsp Tomato Paste

Directions:

1. In a zipper bag, add beef, salt, all-purpose flour, and pepper. Close the bag up and shake it to coat the meat well with the mixture.

2. Select Sear/Sauté mode on the cooker. Melt the butter, and brown the beef on both sides, for 5 minutes.

3. Pour the broth to deglaze the bottom of the pot. Stir in tomato paste, beer, Worcestershire sauce, and the onion soup mix.

4. Close the lid, secure the pressure valve, and select Pressure mode on High pressure for 25 minutes. Press Start/Stop to start cooking.

5. Once the timer is done, do a natural pressure release for 10 minutes, and then a quick pressure release to let out any remaining steam.

6. Open the pressure lid and close the crisping lid. Cook on Broil mode for 10 minutes.

7. Spoon the beef stew into serving bowls and serve with over a bed of vegetable mash with steamed greens.

Nutrition facts Nutrition facts per serving:

Calories 428; Fat 18.2g; Sodium 408mg; Carbs 15.2g; Protein 48.5g

BEEF MEATBALLS IN SPAGHETTI SAUCE

Having a Multicooker without making a meatball sauce is not permissible. You need to make this once and many times for yourself and your guests. Make sure to prepare some squash spaghetti as a side dish for it. I have a recipe shared below to help you in making it.

Preparation Time: 5 minutes | Cooking Time: 11 minutes | Servings: 6

Ingredients:

2 lb Ground Beef

1 cup Breadcrumbs

1 Onion, finely chopped

2 cloves Garlic, minced

Salt and Pepper, to taste

1 tsp dried Oregano

3 tbsp Milk

1 cup Water

1 cup grated Parmesan Cheese

2 Eggs, cracked into a bowl

4 cups Spaghetti Sauce

1 tbsp Olive Oil

Directions:

1. In a bowl, add beef, onion, breadcrumbs, parmesan, eggs, garlic, milk, salt, oregano, and pepper. Mix well with hands and shape bite-size balls.
2. Open the pot, and add the spaghetti sauce, water and the meatballs.
3. Close the lid, secure the pressure valve, and select Steam mode on High pressure for 6 minutes. Press Start/Stop.
4. Once the timer is done, do a natural pressure release for 5 minutes, then do a quick pressure release to let out any extra steam, and open the lid.
5. Dish the meatball sauce over cooked pasta and serve.

Nutrition facts Nutrition facts per serving:

Calories 494; Fat 17.3g; Sodium 329mg; Carbs 18.1g; Protein 47.3g

ORIGINAL BEEF BURGER WITH CHEDDAR

Something very handy to be able to make always. Burgers are a quick way of cooling impromptu hunger pangs, and this recipe makes it tasty enough to make you enjoy every bite.

Preparation Time: 5 minutes | Cooking Time: 15 minutes | Servings: 4

Ingredients:

1 lb Ground Beef

1 (1 oz) packet Dry Onion Soup Mix

1 cup Water

Assembling:

4 Burger Buns

4 Tomato Slices

4 Cheddar Cheese Slices

4 small leaves Lettuce

Mayonnaise

Mustard

Ketchup

Directions:

1. In a bowl, add beef and onion mix, and mix well with hands. Shape in 4 patties and wrap each in foil paper.
2. Pour the water into the inner steel insert of cooker, and fit in the steamer rack. Place the wrapped patties on the trivet, close the lid, and secure the pressure valve, and cook on 10 minutes on Pressure mode on High pressure.
3. Once the timer has stopped, do a natural pressure release for 5 minutes, then a quick pressure release to let out the remaining steam.
4. Use a set of tongs to remove the wrapped beef onto a flat surface and carefully unwrap the patties.
5. To assemble the burgers:
6. In each half of the buns, put a lettuce leaf, then a beef patty, a slice of cheese, and a slice of tomato. Top it with the other halves of buns.
7. Serve with some ketchup, mayonnaise, and mustard.

Nutrition facts Nutrition facts per serving:

Calories 598; Fat 32g; Sodium 370mg; Carbs 35g; Protein 38g

COCONUT BEEF ROAST

To tweak things up from the previous recipe, spice up the beef up with coconut and peanut to for a more exotic aroma. This dish goes well with a side of steamed asparagus and you may have a hot sauce on the side to kick things up.

Preparation Time: 5 minutes | Cooking Time: 35 minutes | Servings: 4

Ingredients:

1 lb Beef Roast, cut into cubes

Salt and Black Pepper to taste

½ cup Coconut Milk, light

½ cup Peanut Satay Sauce

2 cups diced Carrots

Directions:

1. Place the beef inside cooker. In a bowl, mix in coconut milk, salt, pepper, and satay sauce. Pour over the beef. Add the carrots too.
2. Close the lid, secure the pressure valve, and select Pressure mode on High pressure for 15 minutes. Press Start/Stop to start cooking.
3. Once the timer has ended, do a natural pressure release, then a quick pressure release to let out any remaining steam, and open the pot.
4. Give it a stir and close the crisping lid. Cook for 10 minutes on Bake/Roast mode at 400 F.
5. Use a spoon to dish the meat into a serving plate, and serve with a side of steamed greens.

Nutrition facts Nutrition facts per serving:

Calories 483; Fat 27.8g; Sodium 454mg; Carbs 19g; Protein 36.8g

ITALIAN PEPPERONCINI BEEF

Simple, saucy, flavor-packed dish to drool over. Although it takes a bit of time to make, it is worth the effort. Try your hands on this sweet flavored dish and pass the love around.

Preparation Time: 5 minutes | Cooking Time: 50 minutes | Servings: 4

Ingredients:

2 lb Beef Roast, cut into cubes

14 oz jar Pepperoncini Peppers, with liquid

1 pack Brown Gravy Mix

½ cup Water

1 pack Italian Salad Dressing Mix

Directions:

1. Place the beef, pepperoncini peppers, brown gravy mix, Italian salad dressing mix, and water, in cooker's inner pot.
2. Close the lid, secure the pressure valve, and select Pressure mode on High pressure for 35 minutes. Press Start/Stop to start cooking.
3. Once the timer has stopped, do a quick pressure release, and open the pot.
4. Close the crisping lid and cook on Bake/Roast mode for 15 to 20 minutes at 380 F, until nice and tender.
5. When ready, dish the ingredients into a bowl and use two forks to shred the beef. Serve beef sauce in plates with a side of a veggie mash, or bread.

Nutrition facts Nutrition facts per serving:

Calories 415; Fat 18g; Sodium 350mg; Carbs 5g; Protein 47g

SPICY BEEF CHILI WITH WORCESTERSHIRE SAUCE

I honestly can't find the right words to explain the taste of this beef chili. It follows a very simple procedure with ingredients that are very easy to find but yet the blend of juices exuded from the ingredients is mind-blowing.

Preparation Time: 12 minutes | Cooking Time: 28 minutes | Servings: 4

Ingredients:

2 lb Ground Beef

2 tbsp Olive Oil

1 large Red Bell Pepper, chopped

1 large Yellow Bell Pepper, chopped

1 White Onion, Chopped

2 cups Chopped Tomatoes

2 cups Beef Broth

2 Carrots, cut in little bits

2 tsp Onion Powder

2 tsp Garlic Powder

5 tsp Chili Powder

2 tbsp Worcestershire Sauce

2 tsp Paprika

½ tsp Cumin Powder

2 tbsp chopped Parsley

Salt and Black Pepper to taste

Directions:

1. Select Sear/Sauté mode, and add the olive oil and ground beef. Cook the meat until brown, stirring occasionally, for about 8 minutes.
2. Top with the remaining ingredients and mix well. Seal the lid, and cook on Pressure mode on High for 15 minutes. Press Start/Stop to start cooking.
3. Once the timer has ended, do a quick pressure release, and open the lid.
4. Stir the stew and close the crisping lid. Cook on Broil mode for 10 minutes.
5. Dish into serving bowls. Serve this beef chili with crackers or potato mash.

Nutrition facts Nutrition facts per serving:

Calories 437; Fat 18.6g; Sodium 550mg; Carbs 16g; Protein 39.3g

MUSTARDY BEEF BRISKET STEW WITH VEGETABLES

This beef stew is a given when it comes to making awesome stews. The ingredients cook faster in this case especially the beef which cooks so soft to tear apart as you dig your spoon in. Enjoy this stew with the family at dinner; they'll love you without fail.

Preparation Time: 15 minutes | Cooking Time: 55 minutes | Servings: 4

Ingredients:

2 lb Brisket, cut into 2-inch pieces

4 cups Beef Broth

Salt and Black Pepper to taste

1 tbsp Dijon Mustard

1 tbsp Olive Oil

1 lb small Potato, quartered

¼ lb Carrots, cut in 2-inch pieces

1 large Red Onion, quartered

3 cloves Garlic, minced

1 Bay Leaf

2 fresh Thyme sprigs

2 tbsp Cornstarch

3 tbsp chopped Cilantro to garnish

Directions:

1. Pour broth, cornstarch, mustard, ½ teaspoon salt, and ½ teaspoon pepper in a bowl. Whisk them and set aside. Season the beef with salt and pepper.
2. On the cooker, select Sear/Sauté mode.
3. Add the olive oil, and once heated, add the beef strips. Flip halfway through to brown evenly. That should take 7 to 10 minutes.
4. Then, add potato, carrots, onion, garlic, thyme, mustard mixture, and bay leaf. Stir once more. Close the lid, secure the pressure valve, and select Pressure mode on High pressure for 35 minutes. Press Start/Stop.
5. Once the timer has ended, do a quick pressure release.
6. Stir the stew and remove the bay leaf. Season the stew with pepper and salt.
7. Close the crisping lid and cook for 10 minutes on Broil mode. Serve the soup with a bread of your choice.

Nutrition facts Nutrition facts per serving:

Calories 498; Fat 15.2g; Sodium 508mg; Carbs 32.6g; Protein 47.3g

FISH AND SEAFOOD

SPICY AND SWEET MAHI MAHI

It is not surprising that a pretty colored fish like this tastes great in turn. Mahi Mahi works well with different spices, ginger, cumin, fruity flavors, sweet sauce, and peppers. Top with a drizzle of melted butter and the evening will be fulfilling.

Preparation Time: 5 minutes | Cooking Time: 5 minutes | Servings: 4

Ingredients:

4 Mahi Mahi Fillets, fresh

4 cloves Garlic, minced

1 ¼ -inch Ginger, grated

Salt and Black Pepper

2 tbsp Chili Powder

1 tbsp Sriracha Sauce

1 ½ tbsp Maple Syrup

1 Lime, juiced

1 cup Water

Directions:

1. Place mahi mahi on a plate and season with salt and pepper on both sides.
2. In a bowl, add garlic, ginger, chili powder, sriracha sauce, maple syrup, and lime juice. Use a spoon to mix it.
3. With a brush, apply the hot sauce mixture on the fillet.
4. Then, open the cooker's lid, pour the water it and fit the rack at the bottom of the pot. Put the fillets on the trivet.
5. Close the lid, secure the pressure valve, and select Steam mode on High pressure for 5 minutes. Press Start/Stop to start cooking.
6. Once the timer has ended, do a quick pressure release, and open the lid.
7. Use a set of tongs to remove the mahi mahi onto serving plates. Serve with steamed or braised asparagus. For a crispier taste, cook them for 2 minutes on Air Crisp mode, at 300 degrees F.

Nutrition facts Nutrition facts per serving:

Calories 291; Fat 12g; Sodium 280mg; Carbs 20g; Protein 24g

PERNOD MACKEREL & VEGETABLES EN PAPILLOTE

Mackerels are high in omega-3 fatty acids which contain all those good fats that all your body yells for. I love making fish packs because of their exotic feel and the freshness in taste that they come with.

Prep Time: 20 minutes | Cooking Time: 5 minutes + 2 h for marinating | Servings: 6

Ingredients:

3 large Whole Mackerel, cut into 2 pieces

1 pound Asparagus, trimmed

1 Carrot, cut into sticks

1 Celery stalk, cut into sticks

½ cup Butter, at room temperature

6 medium Tomatoes, quartered

1 large Brown Onion, sliced thinly

1 Orange Bell Pepper, seeded and cut into sticks

Salt and Black Pepper to taste

2 ½ tbsp Pernod

3 cloves Garlic, minced

2 Lemons, cut into wedges

1 ½ cups Water

Directions:

1. Cut out 6 pieces of parchment paper a little longer and wider than a piece of fish with kitchen scissors. Then, cut out 6 pieces of foil slightly longer than the parchment papers. Lay the foil wraps on a flat surface and place each parchment paper on each aluminium foil.

2. In a bowl, add tomatoes, onions, garlic, bell pepper, pernod, butter, asparagus, carrot, celery, salt, and pepper. Use a spoon to mix them.

3. Place each fish piece on the layer of parchment and foil wraps. Spoon the vegetable mixture on each fish. Then, wrap the fish and place the fish packets in the refrigerator to marinate for 2 hours. Remove the fish to a flat surface.

4. Open the cooker, pour the water in, and fit the reversible rack at the bottom of the pot. Put the packets on the trivet. Seal the lid and select Steam mode on High pressure for 3 minutes. Press Start/Stop to start cooking.

5. Once the timer has ended, do a quick pressure release, and open the lid.

6. Remove the trivet with the fish packets onto a flat surface. Carefully open the foil and using a spatula. Return the packets to the pot, on top of the rack.

7. Close the crisping lid and cook on Air Crisp for 3 minutes at 300 F. Then, remove to serving plates. Serve with lemon wedges.

Nutrition facts Nutrition facts per serving:

Calories 285; Fat 15.3g; Sodium 44mg; Carbs 15g; Protein 14.9g

STYLISH SCOTTISH SEAFOOD CURRY

I think I got exhausted with having meat curries and though with seafood this time around, the turnout was dope and I know you will say the same. It also gets ready in just 33 minutes rather than 2 hours that it will usually take on the stove top.

Preparation Time: 10 minutes | Cooking Time: 33 minutes | Servings: 8

Ingredients:
Seafood:
½ lb Squid, trimmed and cut into 1-inch rings

½ lb Langoustine Tall Meat

½ lb Scallop Meat

½ lb Mussel Meat

Curry:
4 tbsp Olive Oil

2 cups Shellfish Stock

2 Curry Leaves

2 tbsp Shallot Puree

3 tbsp Yellow Curry Paste

2 tbsp Ginger Paste

2 tbsp Garlic Paste

1 ½ tbsp Chili Powder

1 ½ tbsp Chili Paste

2 tbsp Lemongrass Paste

½ tsp Turmeric Powder

2 tsp Shrimp Powder

1 tsp Shrimp Paste

1 ½ cups Coconut Milk

1 cup Milk

1 tbsp Grants Scotch Whiskey

2 tbsp Fish Curry Powder

Salt to taste

Vegetables:
¼ cup diced Tomatoes

¼ cup chopped Onion

¼ cup chopped Okra

¼ cup chopped Eggplants

Directions:

1. Add olive oil, shallot paste, yellow curry paste, ginger puree, garlic paste, lemongrass paste, chili paste, shrimp paste, and curry leaves.

2. Stir-fry for 10 minutes on Sear/Sauté mode, until well combined and aromatic.

3. Next, add turmeric powder, fish curry powder, and shrimp powder. Stir-fry for another minute. Pour in the shellfish stock and close the crisping lid. Cook on Broil mode for 15 minutes.

4. Open the lid, and add the scallops, squid, chopped onion, okra, tomatoes, and aubergine. Stir lightly.Close the pressure lid, secure the pressure valve, and select Steam mode on High pressure for 5 minutes. Press Start/Stop to start cooking.

5. Once the timer has ended, do a quick pressure release, and open the lid.
6. Add milk, coconut milk, scotch whiskey, and salt. Stir carefully not to mash the aubergine. Select Sear/Sauté and add mussel meat and langoustine. Stir carefully.
7. Simmer the sauce for 3 minutes, press Stop, and turn off the cooker.
8. Dish the seafood with sauce and veggies into serving bowls.
9. Serve with a side of broccoli mash.

Nutrition facts Nutrition facts per serving:
Calories 566; Fat 38g; Sodium 935mg; Carbs 42g; Protein 49g

CREAMY GARLICKY OYSTER STEW

What better way to eat oysters than in a coconut celery fusion. A nutrient-packed stew that you can have with croutons to be filling. Oysters taste good in this delicious sauce, and I will have it over and over again.

Preparation Time: 3 minutes | Cooking Time: 8 minutes | Servings: 4

Ingredients:
2 cups Heavy Cream
2 cups chopped Celery
2 cups Bone Broth
3 (10 oz) jars Shucked Oysters in Liqueur
3 Shallots, minced

3 tbsp Olive Oil
Salt and White Pepper to taste
3 cloves Garlic, minced
3 tbsp chopped Parsley

Directions:
1. Add oil, garlic, shallot, and celery. Stir-fry them for 2 minutes on Sear/Sauté mode, and add the heavy cream, broth, and oysters. Stir once or twice.
2. Close the lid, secure the pressure valve, and select Steam mode on High pressure for 3 minutes. Press Start/Stop.
3. Once the timer has stopped, do a quick pressure release, and open the lid.
4. Season with salt and white pepper. Close the crisping lid and cook for 5 minutes on Broil mode. Stir and dish the oyster stew into serving bowls.
5. Garnish with parsley and top with some croutons.

Nutrition facts Nutrition facts per serving:
Calories 343; Fat 21.2g; Sodium 101mg; Carbs 12g; Protein 17g

ONE-POT MONK FISH WITH POWER GREENS

Luxury in one pot is what this recipe is. It is rich in greens and very good nutrients. For someone like me who is crazy about seafood, I will easily make it my go-to any day and I think you will love it the same way, if not more.

Preparation Time: 7 minutes | Cooking Time: 15 minutes | Servings: 4

Ingredients:

2 tbsp Olive Oil

4 (8 oz) Monk Fish Fillets, cut in 2 pieces each

½ cup chopped Green Beans

2 cloves Garlic, sliced

1 cup Kale Leaves

½ lb Baby Bok Choy, stems removed and chopped largely

1 Lemon, zested and juiced

Lemon Wedges to serve

Salt and White Pepper to taste

Directions:

1. Pour in the coconut oil, garlic, red chili, and green beans. Stir fry for 5 minutes on Sear/Sauté mode.
2. Add the kale leaves, and cook them to wilt, about 3 minutes.
3. Meanwhile, place the fish on a plate and season with salt, white pepper, and lemon zest. After, remove the green beans and kale into a plate and set aside.
4. Back to the pot, add the olive oil and fish. Brown the fillets on each side for about 2 minutes and then add the bok choy in.
5. Pour the lemon juice over the fish and gently stir. Cook for 2 minutes and then press Start/Stop to stop cooking.
6. Spoon the fish with bok choy over the green beans and kale.
7. Serve with a side of lemon wedges and there, you have a complete meal.

Nutrition facts Nutrition facts per serving:

Calories 277; Fat 17g; Sodium 295mg; Carbs 19.4g; Protein 12g

LIME-SAUCY SALMON

Salmon is very good in taste and nutrients. So, in this zingy sauce made to cook in just 5 minutes, I bet you will make it often. Feel free to add a kick of spice to this dish if you will like something hot for the tongue.

Preparation Time: 5 minutes | Cooking Time: 5 minutes | Servings: 4

Ingredients:

4 (5 oz) Salmon Filets

1 cup Water

Salt and Black Pepper to taste

2 tsp Cumin Powder

1 ½ tsp Paprika

2 tbsp chopped Parsley

2 tbsp Olive Oil

2 tbsp Hot Water

1 tbsp Maple Syrup

2 cloves Garlic, minced

1 Lime, juiced

Directions:

1. In a bowl, add cumin, paprika, parsley, olive oil, hot water, maple syrup, garlic, and lime juice. Mix with a whisk. Set aside.
2. Open the cooker and pour the water in. Then, fit the rack. Season the salmon with pepper and salt; and place them on the rack.
3. Close the lid, secure the pressure valve, and select Steam mode on High pressure for 3 minutes. Press Start/Stop.
4. Once the timer has ended, do a quick pressure release, and open the pot.
5. Close the crisping lid and cook on Air Crisp mode for 3 minutes at 300 F.
6. Use a set of tongs to transfer the salmon to a serving plate and drizzle the lime sauce all over it. Serve with steamed swiss chard.

Nutrition facts Nutrition facts per serving:

Calories 564; Fat 32g; Sodium 150mg; Carbs 7g; Protein 64g

FENNEL ALASKAN COD WITH PINTO BEANS

Also known as the Pacific Cod, is a very mild flavored fish and allows all other forms of spices flavor it up just as you will desire. It is one of the best fish on the market to make and passes for a simple dinner or for when you want to impress.

Preparation Time: 4 minutes | Cooking Time: 21 minutes | Servings: 4

Ingredients:

2 (18 oz) Alaskan Cod, cut into 4 pieces each

4 tbsp Olive Oil

2 cloves Garlic, minced

2 small Onions, chopped

½ cup Olive Brine

3 cups Chicken Broth

Salt and Black Pepper to taste

½ cup Tomato Puree

1 head Fennel, quartered

1 cup Pinto Beans, soaked, drained and rinsed

1 cup Green Olives, pitted and crushed

½ cup Basil Leaves

Lemon Slices to garnish

Directions:

1. Heat the olive oil and add the garlic and onion. Stir-fry on Sear/Sauté mode until the onion softens.
2. Pour in chicken broth and tomato puree. Let simmer for about 3 minutes.
3. Add fennel, olives, beans, salt, and pepper. Seal the lid and select Steam mode on High pressure for 10 minutes. Press Start/Stop to start cooking.
4. Once the timer has stopped, do a quick pressure release, and open the lid.
5. Transfer the beans to a plate with a slotted spoon. Adjust broth's taste with salt and pepper and add the cod pieces to the cooker.
6. Close the lid again, secure the pressure valve, and select Steam mode on Low pressure for 3 minutes. Press Start/Stop.
7. Once the timer has ended, do a quick pressure release, and open the lid.
8. Remove the cod into soup plates, top with the beans and basil leaves, and spoon the broth over them.
9. Serve with a side of crusted bread.

Nutrition facts Nutrition facts per serving:

Calories 294; Fat 14.3g; Sodium 240mg; Carbs 26g; Protein 14.82g

CHILI-GARLIC BLACK MUSSELS

When you're done making this dish, you will be as surprised as me when I first saw it too. It is colorful, bursting with flavor, and SUPER tasty. Get on with the fun but don't make it for yourself only.

Preparation Time: 15 minutes | Cooking Time: 30 minutes | Servings: 4

Ingredients:

1 ½ lb Black Mussels, cleaned and de-bearded

3 tbsp Olive Oil

3 large Chilies, seeded and chopped

3 cloves Garlic, peeled and crushed

1 White Onion, chopped finely

10 Tomatoes, skin removed and chopped

4 tbsp Tomato Paste

1 cup Dry White Wine

3 cups Vegetable Broth

⅓ cup fresh Basil Leaves

1 cup fresh Parsley Leaves

Directions:

1. Heat the olive oil on Sear/Sauté mode, and stir-fry the onion, until soft. Add the chilies and garlic, and cook for 2 minutes, stirring frequently.

2. Stir in the tomatoes and tomato paste, and cook for 2 more minutes. Then, pour in the wine and vegetable broth. Let simmer for 5 minutes.

3. Add the mussels, close the lid, secure the pressure valve, and press Steam mode on High pressure for 3 minutes. Press Start/Stop to start cooking.

4. Once the timer has ended, do a natural pressure release for 15 minutes, then a quick pressure release, and open the lid.

5. Remove and discard any unopened mussels. Then, add half of the basil and parsley, and stir. Close the crisping lid and cook on Broil mode for 5 minutes.

6. Dish the mussels with sauce in serving bowls and garnish it with the remaining basil and parsley. Serve with a side of crusted bread.

Nutrition facts Nutrition facts per serving:

Calories 421; Fat 18g; Sodium 630mg; Carbs 23g; Protein 30g

FAMOUS CAROLINA CRAB SOUP

Adding crab to a traditional creamy soup changes the aroma for the better. I pair this soup up with a side of crusted bread and it has never disappointed. Make it during the summer and winter seasons and it will serve just right.

Preparation Time: 5 minutes | Cooking Time: 40 minutes | Servings: 4

Ingredients:

2 lb Crabmeat Lumps

6 tbsp Butter

6 tbsp All-purpose Flour

Salt to taste

1 White Onion, chopped

3 tsp minced Garlic

2 Celery Stalk, diced

1 ½ cup Chicken Broth

¾ cup Heavy Cream

½ cup Half and Half Cream

2 tsp Hot Sauce

3 tsp Worcestershire Sauce

3 tsp Old Bay Seasoning

¾ cup Muscadet

Lemon Juice to serve

Chopped Dill to serve

Directions:

1. Melt the butter on Sear/Sauté mode, and mix in the all-purpose flour, in a fast motion to make a rue. Add celery, onion, and garlic.

2. Stir and cook until soft and crispy, for 3 minutes.

3. While stirring, gradually add the half and half cream, heavy cream, and broth.

4. Let simmer for 2 minutes. Add Worcestershire sauce, old bay seasoning, Muscadet, and hot sauce. Stir and let simmer for 15 minutes. Add the crabmeat and mix it well into the sauce.

5. Close the crisping lid and cook on Broil mode for 10 minutes to soften the meat. Dish into serving bowls, garnish with dill and drizzle squirts of lemon juice over. Serve with a side of garlic crusted bread.

Nutrition facts Nutrition facts per serving:

Calories 478; Fat 24.5g; Sodium 547mg; Carbs 18g; Protein 35.4g

SEARED SCALLOPS WITH BUTTER-CAPER SAUCE

Hanging with your special someone soon? Make this simple seafood to prove your culinary skills. It is so fast in the making, but the pleasant turn out looks better than the time put it.

Preparation Time: 4 minutes | Cooking Time: 12 minutes | Servings: 6

Ingredients:

2 lb Sea Scallops, foot removed

10 tbsp Butter, unsalted

4 tbsp Capers, drained

4 tbsp Olive Oil

1 cup Dry White Wine

3 tsp lemon Zest

Directions:

1. Melt the butter to caramel brown on Sear/Sauté. Use a soup spook to fetch the butter out into a bowl.

2. Next, heat the oil in the pot, once heated add the scallops and sear them on both sides to golden brown which is about 5 minutes.

3. Remove to a plate and set aside.

4. Pour the white wine in the pot to deglaze the bottom while using a spoon to scrape the bottom of the pot of any scallop bits.

5. Add the capers, butter, and lemon zest. Use a spoon to stir the mixture once gently. After 40 seconds, spoon the sauce with capers over the scallops.

6. Serve with a side of braised asparagus.

Nutrition facts Nutrition facts per serving:

Calories 435; Fat 25.8g; Sodium 78mg; Carbs 2g; Protein 32.9g

VEGETABLES & VEGETARIAN

CREAMY BROCCOLI MASH

Make this creamy mash as often as you can to go with the different sauces and meat dishes that are shared here.

Preparation Time: 4 minutes | Cooking Time: 7 minutes | Servings: 4

Ingredients:

3 heads Broccoli, chopped

6 oz Cream Cheese

2 cloves Garlic, crushed

2 tbsp Butter, unsalted

Salt and Black Pepper to taste

2 cups Water

Directions:

1. Turn on the cooker and select Sear/Sauté mode, adjust to High.
2. Drop in the butter, once it melts add the garlic and cook for 30 seconds while stirring frequently to prevent the garlic from burning.
3. Then, add the broccoli, water, salt, and pepper.
4. Close the lid, secure the pressure valve, and select Pressure mode on High pressure for 5 minutes. Press Start/Stop.
5. Once the timer has ended, do a quick pressure release and use a stick blender to mash the ingredients until smooth to your desired consistency and well combined.
6. Stir in Cream cheese. Adjust the taste with salt and pepper. Close the crisping lid and cook for 2 minutes on Broil mode.
7. Serve warm.

Nutrition facts Nutrition facts per serving:

Calories 166; Fat 13g; Sodium 274mg; Carbs 5.6g; Protein 6.7g

SPAGHETTI SQUASH WITH SPINACH-WALNUT PESTO

It serves as spaghetti for when you crave original spaghetti but yet offers all the right nutrition you need. In 6 minutes, this faux spaghetti should be all-ready! Just sprinkle with the amazing Spinach and Walnuts-made Pesto and you'll fall in love with the veggie spaghetti.

Preparation Time: 5 minutes | Cooking Time: 6 minutes | Servings: 4

Ingredients:

4 lb Spaghetti Squash

1 cup Water

For the Pesto

½ cup spinach, chopped

2 tbsp Walnuts

2 Garlic Cloves, minced

Zest and juice from ½ lemon

Salt and ground pepper, to taste

⅓ cup extra virgin olive oil

Directions:

1. In a food processor put all the pesto ingredients and blend until everything is well incorporated. Season to taste and set aside.
2. Put the squash on a flat surface and use a knife to slice in half lengthwise. Scoop out all seeds and discard them.
3. Next, open the cooker, pour the water into it and fit the reversible rack at the bottom. Place the squash halves on the rack, close the lid, secure the pressure valve, and select Steam on High pressure for 5 minutes. Press Start/Stop.
4. Once the timer has ended, do a quick pressure release, and open the lid.
5. Remove the squash halves onto a cutting board and use a fork to separate the pulp strands into spaghetti-like pieces. Return to the pot and close the crisping lid. Cook for 2 minutes on Broil mode.
6. Scoop the spaghetti squash into serving plates and drizzle over the spinach pesto.

Nutrition facts Nutrition facts per serving:

Calories 275; Fat 9.1g; Sodium 330mg; Carbs 46.1g; Protein 5g

CREAMY BUTTERNUT AND CAULIFLOWER SOUP

Super packed with richness: proteins, vitamins, and healthy fats. This soup is so filling and delicious. The toppings make it exciting with a side of toasted bread.

Preparation Time: 15 minutes | Cooking Time: 17 minutes | Servings: 4

Ingredients:

2 tsp Olive Oil

1 large White Onion, chopped

4 cloves Garlic, minced

1 (2 pounds) Butternut Squash, peeled, seeded, and cubed

2 heads Cauliflower, cut in florets

3 cups Chicken Broth

3 tsp Paprika

Salt and Black Pepper to taste

1 cup Milk, full fat

Topping:

Grated Cheddar Cheese, Crumbled Bacon, Chopped Chives, Pumpkin Seeds

Directions:

1. Select Sear/Sauté mode and set to High. Heat olive oil, add the white onion and garlic and sauté for 3 minutes.
2. Next, pour in the butternut squash, cauliflower florets, broth, paprika, pepper, and salt (if needed because of the broth). Stir the ingredients with a spoon.
3. Close the lid, secure the pressure valve, select Pressure mode on High pressure and adjust the time for 8 minutes. Press Start button.
4. Once the timer has ended, do a quick pressure release, and open the lid. Stir in the milk and use a stick blender to puree the soup. Adjust the seasoning.
5. Stir in cheese, close the crisping lid and cook for 2 minutes on Broil mode.
6. Dish the soup into serving bowls. Add the remaining toppings on the soup and serve warm.

Nutrition facts Nutrition facts per serving:

Calories 183; Fat 5.1g; Sodium 485mg; Carbs 23.2g; Protein 10.2g

CRÈME DE LA BROC

I can't get enough of the creamy, tasty goodness that this broccoli soup has to offer. It is farfetched from a pureed green soup but rather the broccoli serves as meat chunks in the soup. You've just gotta-love-it!

Preparation Time: 10 minutes | Cooking Time: 15 minutes | Servings: 6

Ingredients:

3 cups Heavy Cream

3 cups Vegetable Broth

4 tbsp Butter

4 tbsp All-purpose Flour

4 cups chopped Broccoli Florets, only the bushy tops

1 medium Red Onion, chopped

3 cloves Garlic, minced

1 tsp Italian Seasoning

Salt and Black Pepper to taste

1 ½ oz Cream Cheese

1 ½ cups grated Yellow and White Cheddar Cheese + extra for topping

Directions:

1. Select Sear/Sauté mode, adjust to High and melt the butter once the pot is ready. Add the flour and use a spoon to stir until it clumps up. Gradually pour in the heavy cream while stirring until white sauce forms.
2. Fetch out the butter sauce into a bowl and set aside.
3. Press Stop and add the onions, garlic, broth, broccoli, Italian seasoning, and cream cheese. Use a wooden spoon to stir the mixture.
4. Seal the lid, and select Pressure mode on High pressure for 12 minutes. Press Start/Stop. Once the timer has ended, do a quick pressure release.
5. Add in butter sauce and cheddar cheese, salt, and pepper (as necessary). Close the crisping lid and cook on Broil mode for 3 minutes.
6. Dish the soup into serving bowls, top it with extra cheese, to serve.

Nutrition facts Nutrition facts per serving:

Calories 523; Fat 42.5g; Sodium 350mg; Carbs 12.1g; Protein 17.2g

GREEK-STYLE EGGPLANT LASAGNA

This dish poses as a faux lasagna but is cheesy tasty to the core. In 10 minutes or less, it gets ready and is perfect to enjoy by itself, or you may add it as a side to a meat dish. I prefer it to a pork dish.

Preparation Time: 8 minutes | Cooking Time: 18 minutes | Servings: 4

Ingredients:

3 large Eggplants, sliced in uniform ¼ inches

4 ¼ cups Marinara Sauce

1 ½ cups shredded Mozzarella Cheese

Cooking Spray

Chopped Fresh Basil to garnish

¼ cup Parmesan Cheese, grated

Directions:

1. Open the pot and grease it with cooking spray. Arrange the eggplant slices in a single layer on the bottom of the pot and sprinkle some cheese all over it.

2. Arrange another layer of eggplant slices on the cheese, sprinkle this layer with cheese also, and repeat the layering of eggplant and cheese until both ingredients are exhausted.

3. Lightly spray the eggplant with cooking spray and pour the marinara sauce all over it.

4. Close the lid and pressure valve, and select Pressure mode on High pressure for 8 minutes. Press Start/Stop.

5. Once the timer has stopped, do a quick pressure release, and open the lid. Sprinkle with grated parmesan cheese, close the crisping lid and cook for 10 minutes on Bake/Roast mode on 380 degrees F.

6. With two napkins in hand, gently remove the inner pot. Allow cooling for 10 minutes before serving.

7. Garnish the lasagna with basil and serve warm as a side dish.

Nutrition facts Nutrition facts per serving:

Calories 288; Fat 5g; Sodium 407mg; Carbs 38g; Protein 19g

FLAVORFUL LEAFY GREENS

Fun fact here: simple kale, swiss chard, and spinach are given an aromatic kick. With this, your meaty plates just got a lot more pleasant. Make sure to cook them not to be too wilted so that you can enjoy some crunch with as you bite on.

Preparation Time: 2 minutes | Cooking Time: 7 minutes | Servings: 4

Ingredients:

2 lb Baby Spinach

1 lb Kale Leaves

½ lb Swiss Chard

1 tbsp dried Basil

Salt and Black Pepper to season

½ tbsp Butter

½ cup Water

Directions:

1. Turn on the cooker, add the water and fit the reversible rack at the bottom of the pot. Put the spinach, swiss chard, and kale on the rack.

2. Close the lid, secure the pressure valve, and select Steam mode on High pressure for 3 minutes. Press Start/Stop.

3. Once the timer has ended, do a quick pressure release and open the lid.

4. Remove the trivet with the wilted greens onto a plate and discard the water in the pot.

5. Select Sear/Sauté mode on the pot and add the butter. Once it melts, add the spinach and kale back to the pot, and the dried basil. Season with salt and pepper and stir it. Close the crisping lid and cook for 4 minutes on Bake/Roast mode on 380 degrees F.

6. Dish the greens into serving plates and serve as a side dish.

Nutrition facts Nutrition facts per serving:

Calories 130; Fat 3.5g; Sodium 165mg; Carbs 15g; Protein 13g

WINTER CELERIAC PUMPKIN SOUP

Looking for something that is a faux meaty soup? This vegetable soup will work well for you if you are a vegetarian. As you can see from the ingredients, they contain a great macros balance of carbs, fats, and protein.

Preparation Time: 15 minutes | Cooking Time: 13 minutes | Servings: 4

Ingredients:

1 Celeriac, peeled and cubed

16 oz Pumpkin Puree

5 stalks Celery, chopped

1 White Onion, chopped

1 lb Green Beans, cut in 5 to 6 strips each

2 cups Vegetable Broth

3 cups Spinach Leaves

1 tbsp chopped Basil Leaves

¼ tsp dried Thyme

⅛ tsp rubbed Sage

Salt to taste

Directions:

1. Open the cooker and pour in the celeriac, pumpkin puree, celery, onion, green beans, vegetable broth, basil leaves, thyme, sage, and a little salt.
2. Close the lid, secure the pressure valve, and select Steam mode on High pressure for 5 minutes. Press Start/Stop.
3. Once the timer has ended, do a quick pressure release and open the lid.
4. Add in the spinach and stir using a spoon. Close the crisping lid and cook for 3 minutes on Broil mode.
5. Use a soup spoon to fetch the soup into serving bowls.

Nutrition facts Nutrition facts per serving:

Calories 98; Fat 1.5g; Sodium 583mg; Carbs 14.6g; Protein 6.1g

JEWELED QUINOA-STUFFED RED PEPPERS

The Multicooker makes stuffed peppers quickly so why not try this first to give you a hand around the pot if you are new to it? You will enjoy these stuffed peppers!

Preparation Time: 15 minutes | Cooking Time: 25 minutes | Servings: 4

Ingredients:

4 Red Bell Peppers

2 large Tomatoes, chopped

1 small Onion, chopped

2 cloves Garlic, minced

1 tbsp Olive Oil

1 cup Quinoa, rinsed

2 cups Chicken Broth

1 small Zucchini, chopped

1 ½ cup Water

½ tsp Smoked Paprika

½ cup chopped Mushrooms

Salt and Black Pepper to taste

1 cup grated Gouda Cheese

Directions:

1. Select Sear/Sauté mode on High. Once it is ready, add the olive oil to heat and then add the onion and garlic. Sauté for 3 minutes to soften, stirring occasionally.

2. Include the tomatoes, cook for 3 minutes and then add the quinoa, zucchinis, and mushrooms. Season with paprika, salt, and black pepper and stir with a spoon. Cook for 5 to 7 minutes, then, turn the pot off.

3. Use a knife to cut the bell peppers in halves (lengthwise) and remove their seeds and stems. Spoon the quinoa mixture into the bell peppers. Put the peppers in a greased baking dish and pour the broth over.

4. Wipe the pot clean with some paper towels, and pour the water into it. After, fit the steamer rack at the bottom of the pot.

5. Place the baking dish on top of the reversible rack, cover with aluminum foil, close the lid, secure the pressure valve, and select Pressure mode on High pressure for 15 minutes. Press Start/Stop.

6. Once the timer has ended, do a quick pressure release and open the lid. Remove the aluminum foil and sprinkle with the gouda cheese. Close the crisping lid, select Bake/Roast mode and cook for 10 minutes on 375 degrees F.

7. Arrange the stuffed peppers on a serving platter and serve right away or as a side to a meat dish.

Nutrition facts Nutrition facts per serving:

Calories 409; Fat 16.9g; Sodium 240mg; Carbs 42g; Protein 19.8g

SPICY ZOODLE AND BOK CHOY SOUP

This green zoodle soup satisfies me in tastes, nutrients, and flavor and is even healthier than the usual noodle soup.

Preparation Time: 15 minutes | Cooking Time: 17 minutes | Servings: 6

Ingredients:

1 lb Baby Bok Choy, stems removed

6 oz Shitake Mushrooms, stems removed and sliced to a 2-inch thickness

3 Carrots, peeled and sliced diagonally

2 Zucchinis, spiralized

2 Sweet Onion, chopped

2-inch Ginger, chopped

2 cloves Garlic, peeled

2 tbsp Sesame Oil

2 tbsp Soy Sauce

2 tbsp Chili Paste

6 cups Water

Salt to taste

Chopped Green Onion to garnish

Sesame Seeds to garnish

Directions:

1. In a food processor, add the chili paste, ginger, onion, and garlic; and process them until they are pureed.
2. Turn on the cooker and select Sear/Sauté mode to High.
3. Pour in the sesame oil, once it has heated add the onion puree and cook for 3 minutes while stirring constantly to prevent burning. Add the water, mushrooms, soy sauce, and carrots.
4. Close the lid, secure the pressure valve, and select Pressure mode on High pressure for 5 minutes. Press Start/Stop.
5. Once the timer has ended, do a quick pressure release and open the lid.
6. Add the zucchini noodles and bok choy, and stir to ensure that they are well submerged in the liquid.
7. Adjust the taste with salt, cover the pot with the crisping lid, and let the vegetables cook for 10 minutes on Broil mode.
8. Use a soup spoon to dish the soup with veggies into soup bowls.
9. Sprinkle with green onions and sesame seeds.
10. Serve as a complete meal.

Nutrition facts Nutrition facts per serving:

Calories 115; Fat 6.1g; Sodium 46mg; Carbs 15g; Protein 2.1g

MEATLESS CHIPOTLE CHILE WITH WALNUTS

Nothing hurts to tweak an ordinary vegetable chili with some nutty flavor. In here, it is packed with rich tastes and aromas to go with a zoodle, turnip mash or steamed greens dish. Have fun indulging in the aromas and enjoy the good taste.

Preparation Time: 10 minutes | Cooking Time: 22 minutes | Servings: 4

Ingredients:

4 Celery Stalks, chopped

2 (15 oz) cans Diced Tomatoes

1 tbsp Olive Oil

3 Carrots, chopped

2 cloves Garlic, minced

2 tsp Smoked Paprika

2 Green Bell Pepper, diced

½ cup Water

1 tbsp Cinnamon Powder

1 tbsp Cumin Powder

1 Sweet Onion, chopped

2 cups Tomato Sauce

1.5 oz Dark Chocolate, chopped

1 small Chipotle, minced

1 ½ cups raw Walnuts, chopped + extra to garnish

Salt and Pepper, to taste

Chopped Cilantro to garnish

Directions:

1. Turn on the cooker, open the lid and select Sear/Sauté mode on Medium.
2. Pour in the oil to heat and add the onion, celery, and carrots. Sauté for 4 minutes. Add the garlic, cumin, cinnamon, and paprika. Stir and let the sauce cook for 2 minutes.
3. Now, include the bell peppers, tomatoes, tomato sauce, chipotle, water, and walnuts Stir.
4. Close the lid, secure the pressure valve, and select Pressure mode on High pressure for 15 minutes. Press Start/Stop.
5. Once the timer has ended, do a quick pressure release, and open the lid.
6. Pour the chopped chocolate in and stir it until it melts and is well incorporated into the chili. Adjust the taste with salt and pepper. Close the crisping lid and cook for 5 minutes on Broil mode.
7. Dish the chili into a serving bowl, garnish it with the remaining walnuts and cilantro. Serve with some noodles.

Nutrition facts Nutrition facts per serving:

Calories 387; Fat 25.7g; Sodium 222mg; Carbs 42g; Protein 15g

KOREAN-STYLE TOFU NODDLE SOUP

Tofu is an all-time vegetarian favorite, and I possibly couldn't leave out a delicious recipe of it. So cheers to a happy moment making this delicious tofu soup. Before you begin, know that this soup is very aromatic and you could be found guilty of having too much of it.

Preparation Time: 10 minutes | Cooking Time: 15 minutes | Servings: 4

Ingredients:

16 oz firm Tofu, water- packed

7 cloves Garlic, minced

2 tbsp Korean red pepper flakes (gochugaru)

1 tbsp Sugar

1 tbsp Olive Oil

2 tbsp Ginger Paste

¼ cup Soy Sauce

3 cup sliced Bok Choy

6 ounces dry Egg Noodles

4 cups Vegetable Broth

1 cup sliced Shitake Mushrooms

½ cup chopped Cilantro

Directions:

1. Drain the liquid out of the tofu, pat the tofu dry with paper towels, and use a knife to cut them into 1-inch cubes.
2. Turn your cooker on and select Sear/Sauté mode on Medium.
3. Pour the oil to heat, add the garlic and ginger, and sauté for 2 minutes.
4. Add the sugar, broth, and soy sauce. Stir and cook for 30 seconds. Include the tofu and bok choy, close the lid, secure the pressure valve, and select Pressure mode on High pressure for 10 minutes. Press Start/Stop.
5. Once the timer has ended, do a quick pressure release and open the lid. Add the zucchini noodles, give it a good stir using a spoon, and close the crisping lid. Let the soup cook for 4 minutes on Broil mode. Use a soup spoon to fetch the soup into soup bowls, top with cilantro and enjoy.

Nutrition facts Nutrition facts per serving:

Calories 354; Fat 15g; Sodium 489mg; Carbs 41.7g; Protein 21.2g

RESTAURANT-STYLE PARMESAN STUFFED MUSHROOMS

Who says you can't have stuffed mushrooms without meat. Right here, this has been proven! It gets ready in 12 minutes and the chewy texture that comes with it is what will make you have it for days.

Preparation Time: 15 minutes | Cooking Time: 12 minutes | Servings: 4

Ingredients:

10 large White Mushrooms, stems removed

¼ cup Roasted Red Bell Peppers, chopped

1 Red Bell Pepper, seeded and chopped

1 Green Onion, chopped

1 small Onion, chopped

¼ cup grated Parmesan Cheese

½ cup Water

1 tbsp Butter

½ tsp dried Oregano

Salt and Black Pepper to taste

Directions:

1. Turn on the cooker and select Sear/Sauté mode on Medium.
2. Put in the butter to melt and add the roasted and fresh peppers, green onion, onion, oregano, salt, and pepper. Use a spoon to mix and cook for 2 minutes.
3. Spoon the bell pepper mixture into the mushrooms and use a paper towel to wipe the pot and place the stuffed mushrooms in it, 5 at a time. Pour in water.
4. Close the lid, secure the pressure valve, and select pressure mode on High pressure for 5 minutes. Press Start/Stop.
5. Once the timer has ended, do a quick pressure release and open the lid.
6. Sprinkle with parmesan cheese and close the crisping lid. Select Bake/Roast, adjust the temperature to 380 degrees F and the time to 2 minutes and press
7. Start/Stop button.
8. Use a set of tongs to remove the stuffed mushrooms onto a plate and repeat the cooking process for the remaining mushrooms.
9. Serve hot with a side of steamed green veggies and a sauce.

Nutrition facts Nutrition facts per serving:

Calories 80; Fat 4g; Sodium 190mg; Carbs 8g; Protein 5g

WINTER MINESTRONE SOUP

Remember to make this sauce as a saver for the cold nights. You can add a shake of hot sauce to it but most importantly, serve it warm to have the best satisfaction.

Preparation Time: 15 minutes | Cooking Time: 12 minutes | Servings: 4

Ingredients:

1 (15.5 oz) can Cannellini Beans

1 Potato, peeled and diced

1 Carrot, peeled and chopped

1 cup chopped Butternut Squash

2 small Red Onions, cut in wedges

1 cup chopped Celery

1 tbsp chopped Fresh Rosemary

8 Sage Leaves, chopped finely

1 Bay Leaf

4 cups Vegetable Broth

Salt and Pepper, to taste

2 tsp Olive Oil

2 tbsp chopped fresh Parsley

Directions:

1. Add the potato, carrot, squash, onion, celery, rosemary, sage leaves, bay leaf, vegetable broth, salt, pepper, and olive oil to the pot of your cooker.

2. Close the lid, secure the pressure valve, and select Pressure mode on High pressure for 7 minutes. Press Start/Stop.

3. Once the timer has ended, do a quick pressure release and open the lid. Add the cannellini beans and stir with a spoon. Close the crisping lid and cook for 5 minutes on Broil mode.

4. Use a soup spoon to fetch the soup into soup bowls. Garnish with fresh parsley and serve with a side of crusted bread.

Nutrition facts Nutrition facts per serving:

Calories 198; Fat 4.45g; Sodium 583mg; Carbs 27g; Protein 4.12g

STEAMED ASPARAGUS WITH PINE NUTS

Steamed asparagus bring a worth of taste to the plate, and they go well with almost any stew or chili that you can think of. There are quite a number of these shared under the stew section, feel free to do yourself some good.

Preparation Time: 2 minutes | Cooking Time: 11 minutes | Servings: 4

Ingredients:

1 ½ lb Asparagus, ends trimmed

Salt and Pepper, to taste

1 cup Water

1 tbsp butter

½ cup chopped Pine Nuts

1 tbsp Olive Oil to garnish

Directions:

1. Open the cooker, pour the water in, and fit the reversible rack at the bottom.
2. Place the asparagus on the rack, close the crisping lid, select Air Crisp mode, and set the time to 8 minutes on 380 degrees F. Press Start/Stop.
3. At the 4-minute mark, carefully turn the asparagus over.
4. When ready, remove to a plate, sprinkle with salt and pepper, and set aside.
5. Select Sear/Sauté on your cooker, set to Medium and melt the butter.
6. Add the pine nuts and cook for 2-3 minutes until golden. Scatter over the asparagus the pine nuts, and drizzle olive oil.

Nutrition facts Nutrition facts per serving:

Calories 182; Fat 15g; Sodium 296mg; Carbs 13g; Protein 7g

FALL PORTOBELLO MUSHROOM PILAF

Fall is time to enjoy some tasty mushroomy pilaf. I reckon it will satisfy hunger pangs at the right moments.

Preparation Time: 5 minutes | Cooking Time: 10 minutes | Servings: 4

Ingredients:

2 cups Brown Rice, rinsed

4 cups Vegetable Broth

3 teaspoons Olive oil

1 cup Portobello Mushrooms, thinly sliced

¼ cup Romano Cheese, grated

Salt to taste

2 sprigs Parsley, to garnish

Directions:

1. Heat the oil on Sear/Sauté on Medium, and stir-fry the mushrooms for 3 minutes until golden. Season with salt, and add rice and broth.
2. Close the lid, secure the pressure valve, and select Pressure mode on High pressure for 5 minutes. Press Start/Stop to start cooking.
3. Once the timer has ended, do a quick pressure release and open the lid.
4. Spread the cheese over and close the crisping lid. Select Bake/Roast, adjust to 375 degrees F and the timer to 2 minutes. Press Start/Stop to start cooking.
5. To serve, plate the pilaf and top with freshly chopped parsley.

Nutrition facts Nutrition facts per serving:

Calories 417; Fat 16.9g; Sodium 198mg; Carbs 61.8g; Protein 12.1g

CREAMY AND GREENY SOUP

You will be surprised at the turn out of this kale blend. I never thought kale could taste this good until this recipe came about. I like very creamy stuff, so I take hold of the opportunity to make it creamy good and I think you will like it if you do same.

Preparation Time: 8 minutes | Cooking Time: 13 minutes | Servings: 4

Ingredients:

½ lb Kale Leaves, chopped

½ lb Spinach Leaves, chopped

½ lb Swiss Chard Leaves, chopped

1 tbsp Olive Oil

1 Onion, chopped

4 cloves Garlic, minced

4 cups Vegetable Broth

1 ¼ cup Heavy Cream

Salt and Pepper, to taste

1 ½ tbsp. White Wine Vinegar

Chopped Peanuts to garnish

Directions:

1. Turn on the cooker and select Sear/Sauté mode on Medium.
2. Add the olive oil, once it has heated add the onion and garlic and sauté for 2-3 minutes until soft. Add greens and vegetable broth.
3. Close the lid, secure the pressure valve, and select Pressure mode on High pressure for 10 minutes. Press Start/Stop.
4. Once the timer has ended, do a quick pressure release.
5. Add the white wine vinegar, salt, and pepper. Use a stick blender to puree the ingredients in the pot. Close the crisping lid and cook for 3 minutes on Broil mode. Stir in the heavy cream.
6. Spoon the soup into bowls, sprinkle with peanuts, and serve.

Nutrition facts Nutrition facts per serving:

Calories 269; Fat 14.2g; Sodium 431mg; Carbs 14.3g; Protein 12.5g

DESSERTS

VANILLA-CINNAMON BALLS

These scrumptious bites are perfect when hosting big numbers at a party. I enjoyed similar bites as a child, so I decided to make them, but in this case, they are made with wheat flour and tossed in cinnamon-sugar afterward. Serve them with tea or with any drink that you like.

Preparation Time: 10 minutes | Cooking Time: 10 minutes | Servings: 4

Ingredients

⅔ cup all-purpose flour

½ teaspoon baking powder

3 tablespoons white sugar

1 tbsp ground cinnamon

A pinch of salt

2 tbsp cold butter, cubed

¼ cup sour cream

1 tbsp vanilla powder

Cooking spray

Directions

1. Mix the all-purpose flour, baking powder, 1 tablespoon of sugar, ¼ teaspoon of cinnamon, and the salt in a medium bowl.

2. Add the butter and use a pastry cutter to cut into the butter to be broken into pieces. Pour in the sour cream and mix until the dough forms into a ball.

3. Knead the dough on a flat surface until a smooth both is achieved. Divide the dough into 8 pieces and roll each piece into a ball.

4. Coat the preheated Cook & Crisp basket with cooking spray. Put the balls in the basket with space in between each ball and oil the balls with cooking spray.

5. Close the crisping lid. Choose Air Crisp, set the temperature to 350 degrees F, and set the time to 10 minutes. Press Start/Stop.

6. In a medium mixing bowl, combine the remaining sugar and cinnamon, and vanilla powder.

7. When done baking, toss the dough balls in the vanilla-cinnamon and sugar mixture.

Nutrition facts per serving:

Calories 167; Fat 7g; Sodium 331mg; Carbohydrates: 25g; Protein 3g

BLUEBERRY PIES

Hand pies are convenient and one of the tastiest treats that ever happened to America. These ones are stuffed with a sweet, syrupy apple filling and encased in baked piecrusts. Unlike, regular apple pies that break apart once spooned onto the serving plate; these are intact given you more control of the pie.

Preparation Time: 15 minutes | Cooking Time: 12 minutes | Servings: 4

Ingredients

1 cup blueberries
2 tablespoons sugar
½ lemon, juiced
¼ teaspoon salt
½ teaspoon vanilla extract
½ teaspoon cornstarch
4 frozen piecrusts; thawed
Nonstick cooking spray

Directions

1. In a large mixing bowl, combine the blueberries, sugar, lemon juice, salt, and vanilla. Allow the mixture to stand for 10 minutes, then drain, and reserve 1 tablespoon of the liquid.
2. In a small bowl, whisk the cornstarch into the reserved liquid and then, mix with the blueberry mixture.
3. Put the piecrusts on a lightly floured surface and cut into 4. Spoon a tablespoon of blueberry mixture in the center of the circle, with ½ an inch's border around the dough. Brush the edges with water and fold the dough over the filling. Press the edges with a fork to seal.
4. Cut 3 small slits on top of each pie and oil with cooking spray. Arrange the pies in a single layer in the basket.
5. Close the crisping lid, choose Air Crisp, set the temperature to 350 degrees F, and set the time to 12 minutes. Press Start/Stop to begin baking.
6. Once done baking, remove, and place the pies on a wire rack to cool.

Nutrition facts per serving:

Calories 298; Fat 15g; Sodium 307mg; Carbs 40g; Protein 2g

RASPBERRY CRUMBLE CAKE

I like the redness that appears when this crumble is spooned into, sending reminders of summer. I chose to keep the filling simple here with only raspberries; however, the good thing with crumbles is that you can mix and match fruits per season to keep you in time's mood.

Preparation Time: 10 minutes | Cooking Time: 20 minutes | Servings: 6

Ingredients

- 2 cups frozen raspberries
- 2 tbsp cornstarch
- ½ cup water
- 1 teaspoon lemon juice
- ½ cup all-purpose flour
- 1 cup brown sugar
- ½ cup rolled oats
- ⅓ cup cold unsalted butter, cut into pieces
- 1 teaspoon cinnamon powder

Directions

1. Add the raspberries in a cake pan.
2. In a small mixing bowl, combine the cornstarch, 1 tablespoon of water, lemon juice, and 3 tablespoons of sugar. Pour the mixture all over the raspberries.
3. Put the reversible rack in the pot. Cover the pan with foil and pour the remaining water into the pot. Put the pan on the rack.
4. Seal the pressure lid, choose Pressure, set to High, and set the time to 10 minutes, then choose Start/Stop.
5. In a medium bowl, mix the flour, remaining sugar, oats, butter, and cinnamon, until a crumble forms.
6. When done pressure-cooking, do a quick pressure release and carefully open the lid.
7. Remove the foil and stir the fruit mixture. After, spread the crumble evenly on the berries.
8. Close the crisping lid; choose Air Crisp, set the temperature to 400 degrees F, and the time to 10 minutes. Choose Start/Stop to begin crisping. Cook until the top has browned and the fruit is bubbling.
9. When done baking, remove the rack with the pan from the pot, and serve.

Nutrition facts per serving:

Calories 396; Fat 12g; Sodium 142mg; Carbs 72g; Protein 4g

NEW YORK CHEESECAKE WITH STRAWBERRIES

Get me a cheesecake for any occasion, and I will be very grateful. And this makes me pretty particular about the kind of cheesecake I eat. Anyway, just like the regular, this recipe fills a biscuit crust with cream cheese filling and left as simple as that so that you have the flexibility to top it with anything that you like.

Preparation Time: 15 minutes | Cooking Time: 35 minutes | Servings: 6

Ingredients

Cooking spray

1½ cups finely crushed graham crackers

2 tablespoons sugar

4 tbsp butter, melted

16 ounces cream cheese, softened

½ cup brown sugar

¼ cup sour cream

1 tablespoon all-purpose flour

1½ teaspoons vanilla extract

½ teaspoon salt

2 eggs

1 cup water

Fresh Strawberries, cut in half lengthwise for garnish

Directions

1. Line a cake pan with parchment paper and grease with cooking spray the paper

2. In a medium mixing bowl, mix the graham cracker crumbs, sugar, and butter. Spoon the mixture into the pan and press firmly into with a spoon.

3. In a deep bowl and with a hand mixer, beat the beat the cream cheese and brown sugar until well-mixed. Whisk in the sour cream to be smooth and stir in the flour, vanilla, and salt.

4. Crack the eggs in and beat but not to be overly smooth. Pour the mixture into the pan over the crumbs.

5. Next, pour the water into the pot. Put the pan on the reversible rack and put the rack in the pot. Seal the pressure lid, choose Pressure, set to High, and set the time to 35 minutes. Choose Start/Stop.

6. Once done baking, perform a natural pressure release for 10 minutes. Carefully open the lid.

7. Remove the pan from the rack and allow the cheesecake to cool for 1 hour. Cover the cheesecake with foil and chill in the refrigerator for 4 hours to serve. Decorate with strawberry halves.

Nutrition facts per serving:

Calories 551; Fat 39g; Sodium 627mg; Carbs 43g; Protein 9g

BERRY COBBLER WITH CINNAMON-CREAM TOPPING

I enjoy fruit cobblers a lot; I make them with peaches, or different types of berries or just a mixture of both. It is a delight to scoop through a crusty, crispy topping into softened berries that taste out of this world. For sweeter tastes, sprinkle the top with sugar, and serve warm.

Preparation Time: 10 minutes | Cooking Time: 15 minutes | Servings: 4

Ingredients

2½ cups frozen mixed berries

3 tablespoons cornstarch

1 cup sugar

FOR THE TOPPING

1 cup flour

¼ teaspoon cinnamon powder

5 tablespoons powdered sugar, divided

⅔ cup crème fraiche, plus more as needed

1 tablespoon melted unsalted butter

1 tablespoon whipping cream

Directions

1. Pour the blackberries into the inner pot along with the cornstarch and sugar. Mix to combine.

2. Seal the pressure lid, choose Pressure; adjust the pressure to High and the cook time to 3 minutes. Press Start.

3. After cooking, perform a quick pressure release and carefully open the lid.

4. For the topping, in a small bowl, whisk the flour, cinnamon powder, and 3 tablespoons of sugar. In a separate small bowl, whisk the crème fraiche with the melted butter. Pour the cream mixture on the dry Ingredients and combine evenly.

5. Spoon 2 to 3 tablespoons of dough on top over the berries and spread out slightly on top. Brush the topping with the whipping cream and sprinkle with the remaining sugar.

6. Close the crisping lid and choose Bake/Roast; adjust the temperature to 325 degrees F and the cook time to 12 minutes. Press Start.

7. When ready, the topping should be cooked through and lightly browned. Allow cooling before slicing.

Nutrition facts per serving:

Calories 523; Fat 9g; S Sodium 39mg; Carbs 109g; Protein 6g

WHITE CHOCOLATE CHEESECAKE

Even when I'm tummy full, with this cheesecake in my face, I confess I will still take a bite or two. It is a good way to combine white chocolate with vanilla, which is swirled to be pretty and inviting at the top. Enjoy the crispy, creamy beauty!

Preparation Time: 10 minutes | Cooking Time: 31 minutes | Servings: 8

Ingredients

- 4 ounces graham crackers, crushed
- 2 tablespoons unsalted butter, melted
- 16 ounces cream cheese, room temperature
- ½ cup sugar
- 2 tablespoons heavy cream
- 2 teaspoons vanilla extract
- 2 tablespoons sour cream
- 2 large eggs
- 3 ounces white chocolate chips, melted

Directions

1. In a small bowl, mix the cookie crumbs and butter. Spoon the crumbs into a spring form pan and press all around with a spoon. Place the reversible rack in the inner pot and put the spring form pan on top.
2. Close the crisping lid and choose Air Crisp; adjust the temperature to 350 degrees F and the cook time to 6 minutes. Press Start and bake until fragrant and set. Remove the pan and let the crumbs cool.
3. In a medium bowl and using a hand mixer, beat the cream cheese until smooth, add the sugar, and beat further until smooth. Pour in the heavy cream, vanilla extract, and sour cream. Whisk again and crack the eggs into the bowl one after the other while whisking after each egg is added.
4. Spoon ½ cup of the cream mixture into a bowl and mix in the chocolate chips.
5. Pour the remaining cream mixture into the spring form pan, drop spoonfuls of the chocolate mixture with even distance on the filling and run the tip of a skewer through each chocolate drop to marbleize the top of the filling. Cover the filling with aluminium foil. Pour 1 cup of water into the inner pot. Fix in the reversible rack in the pot and put the spring form pan on top.
6. Seal the pressure lid, choose Pressure; adjust the pressure to High and the cook time to 25 minutes. Press Start. After cooking, perform a natural pressure release for 10 minutes. Take off the foil. Chill the cheesecake before serving.

Nutrition facts per serving:

Calories 428; Fat 32g; Sodium 285mg; Carbs 30g; Protein 7g

CHOCOLATE BROWNIES WITH DULCE DE LECHE

What's wrong with spoiling yourself with a sweet, nutty brownie? These ones are worth been spoiled for. The brownies are topped with a good drizzle of caramel and toasted crunchy walnuts that will make you feel like a child again.

Preparation Time: 10 minutes | Cooking Time: 54 minutes | Servings: 4

Ingredients

8 ounces dark chocolate

8 tablespoons unsalted butter

1 cup sugar

2 teaspoons almond extract

A pinch of salt

2 large eggs, at room temperature

¾ cup flour

Cooking spray

½ cup dulce de leche

½ cup toasted walnuts

Directions

1. Put the chocolate and butter in a small bowl and pour 1 cup of water into the inner pot. Place the reversible rack in the lower position of the pot and put the bowl on top.

2. Close the crisping lid, choose Bake/Roast; adjust the temperature to 375 degrees F and the cook time to 10 minutes to melt the chocolate and butter. Press Start. Check after 5 minutes and stir. Remove the bowl from the pot.

3. Use a small spatula to transfer the chocolate mixture into a medium bowl and stir in the almond extract, sugar, and salt. One after another, crack each egg into the bowl and whisk after each addition.

4. Mix in the flour until smooth, about 1 minute.

5. Grease a round cake pan with cooking spray. Pour the batter into the prepared pan and place on the rack.

6. Close the crisping lid and choose Bake/Roast; adjust the temperature to 250 degrees F and the cook time to 40 minutes. Press Start. Once the time is up, open the lid.

7. Generously drizzle the dulce de leche on top of the brownies and scatter the walnuts on top. Close the crisping lid again and adjust the temperature to 325 degrees F and the cook time to 4 minutes. Press Start.

8. Allow the brownies cool and serve

Nutrition facts per serving:

Calories 1054; Fat 59g; Sodium 193mg; Carbs 123g; Protein 12g

EASY CRÈME BRULEE

I love crème brulee so much that it is my first choice dessert to pick when at the restaurant. Being able to make it quickly with the Multicooker is very exciting so cheers to many days of CRÈME BRULÉE.

Preparation Time: 5 minutes | Cooking Time: 23 minutes + 6 hours of cooling | Servings: 4

Ingredients:

3 cups Heavy Whipping Cream

6 tbsp Sugar

7 large Egg Yolks

2 tbsp Vanilla Extract

2 cups Water

Directions:

1. In a mixing bowl, add the yolks, vanilla, whipping cream, and half of the swerve sugar. Use a whisk to mix them until they are well combined.
2. Pour the mixture into the ramekins and cover them with aluminium foil.
3. Open the cooker, fit the reversible rack into the pot, and pour in the water.
4. Place 3 ramekins on the rack and place the remaining ramekins to sit on the edges of the ramekins below.
5. Close the lid, secure the pressure valve, and select Pressure mode on High for 8 minutes. Press Start/Stop.
6. Once the timer has stopped, do a natural pressure release for 10 minutes, then a quick pressure release to let out the remaining pressure.
7. With a napkin in hand, remove the ramekins onto a flat surface and then into a refrigerator to chill for at least 6 hours.
8. After refrigeration, remove the ramekins and remove the aluminium foil.
9. Equally, sprinkle the remaining sugar on it and return to the pot. Close the csisping lid, select Bake/Roast mode, set the timer to 4 minutes on 380 degrees F. Serve the crème brulee chilled with whipped cream.

Nutrition facts Nutrition facts per serving:

Calories 487; Fat 42.1g; Sodium 38mg; Carbs 23.2g; Protein 5.1g

RASPBERRY TART WITH VANILLA CREAM CHEESE FILLING

A tart that surely impresses guest so make it when you have your next troop of guests coming over. Piecrust cooks to be soft within and crunchy on the sides and then filled with a sweet, creamy filling. Afterward, a generous topping of raspberries is spooned over. It is one for the present and the future, you should teach the kids to make them.

Preparation Time: 20 minutes | Cooking Time: 20 minutes | Servings: 4

Ingredients

1 frozen piecrust, thawed

2½ cups fresh raspberries, divided

1 tablespoon arrowroot starch

2 tablespoons water

¼ cup sugar

¼ teaspoon grated lemon zest

1 teaspoon freshly squeezed lemon juice

Pinch salt

FOR THE CREAM FILLING

1 teaspoon vanilla extract

8 ounces cream cheese, at room temperature

½ cup confectioners' sugar

¼ cup heavy (whipping) cream

Directions

1. Roll out the pie crust and fit into a tart pan. Use a fork to prick all over the bottom of the dough. Place the reversible rack in the pot and put the tart pan on top.

2. Close the crisping lid, choose Bake/Roast; adjust the temperature to 250 degrees F and the cook time to 15 minutes. Press Start.

3. When done baking, open the lid and check the crust. It should be set and lightly brown around the edges. Close the crisping lid again. Adjust the temperature to 375 F and the cook time to 4 minutes. Press Start. Set the crust aside to cool.

4. Fetch out 1 cup of berries into the inner pot. In a small bowl, whisk the arrowroot starch and water until smoothly mixed. Pour the slurry on the raspberries along with the sugar, lemon zest, lemon juice, and salt. Mix to distribute the slurry among the raspberries. Seal the pressure lid, choose Pressure; adjust the pressure to High and the cook time to 2 minutes. Press Start.

5. Once done cooking, perform a quick pressure release and carefully open the lid. Add the remaining 1½ cups of raspberries, stirring to coat with the cooked mixture. Then, allow cooling.

6. In a bowl and with a hand mixer, whisk the vanilla extract and cream cheese until evenly combined and smooth.

7. Mix in the confectioners' sugar and whisk again until the sugar has fully incorporated and the mixture is light and smooth. With clean whisks and in

another bowl, beat the heavy cream until soft peaks form. Fold the heavy cream into the vanilla mixture. Spoon the cream filling into the piecrust and scatter the remaining raspberries on the cream. Chill for 30 minutes before serving.

Nutrition facts per serving:

Calories 664; Fat 40g; Sodium 421mg; Carbs 74g; Protein 6g

HOT LAVA CAKE

Got a big group to serve? This drool deserving cake will go around well while satisfying everyone. The amazing thing about it is that it needs just six (6) ingredients to get ready.

Preparation Time: 10 minutes | Cooking Time: 29 minutes | Servings: 8

Ingredients:

1 cup Butter

4 tbsp Milk

4 tsp Vanilla Extract

1 ½ cups Chocolate Chips

1 ½ cups Sugar

Powdered sugar to garnish

7 tbsp All-purpose Flour

5 Eggs

1 cup Water

Directions:

1. Grease the cake pan with cooking spray and set aside. Open the cooker, fit the reversible rack at the bottom of it, and pour in the water.

2. In a medium heatproof bowl, add the butter and chocolate and melt them in the microwave for about 2 minutes. Remove it from the microwave. Add sugar and stir well. Add the eggs, milk, and vanilla extract and stir again. Finally, add the flour and stir until smooth. Pour the batter into the greased cake pan and use the spatula to level it.

3. Place the pan on the trivet in the pot, close the lid, secure the pressure valve, select Pressure on High for 15 minutes. Press Start/Stop. Once the timer has gone off, do a natural pressure release for 10 minutes.

4. Remove the pan to a flat surface. Put a plate over the pan and flip the cake over into the plate. Pour the powdered sugar in a fine sieve and sift it over the cake. Use a knife to cut the cake into 8 slices and serve immediately (while warm).

Nutrition facts Nutrition facts per serving:

Calories 460; Fat 23g; Sodium 240mg; Carbs 28g; Protein 9.5g

HOLIDAY CHOCOLATE CHEESECAKE

This is a kiddie special, and I bet that they will be all over you when you make them. The good thing is that you can make this dessert often for the entire family because it is made of healthy, non-fattening ingredients.

Preparation Time: 15 minutes | Cooking Time: 25 minutes + 6 hours for cooling | Servings: 8

Ingredients:

2 cups Water

Crust:

1 cup Graham Crackers Crumbs

1 tbsp Sugar

3 tbsp Cocoa Powder

3 tbsp Butter, melted

Filling:

2 Eggs, room temperature, cracked

2 Egg Yolks, room temperature, cracked

20 oz Cream Cheese, room temperature

½ cup Granulated Sugar

½ cup Cocoa Powder

1 cup Heavy Cream

½ cup Sour Cream

2 tsp Vanilla Extract

8 oz Baking Chocolate, melted

Directions:

1. Line a cake pan with parchment paper.
2. In a mixing bowl, add the graham crackers crumbs, cocoa powder, and sugar. Mix evenly then add the melted butter and mix again until well incorporated.
3. Spoon the mixture into the pan and tap it to firm using the spoon. Set aside.
4. Using an electric mixer, beat the cream cheese and cocoa powder. While still mixing, add the eggs and egg yolks. Once combined and still mixing, add the sour cream, melted chocolate, heavy cream, and vanilla extract. Scrape the sides of the bowl as you mix. Once well combined, turn off the electric mixer, and spoon the filling mixture onto the crust in the springform pan. Use the spatula to smoothen it out.
5. Open the cooker, and fit the rack at the bottom of it and pour in the water.
6. Cover the pan with foil and place on the reversible rack. Close the lid, select pressure mode on High pressure for 25 minutes. Press Start/Stop.
7. Once the timer has stopped, do a natural pressure release for 10 minutes, then a quick pressure release to let out the remaining steam.
8. With napkins in both hands, hold the trivet's sling and lift it out with the spring form pan. Let the cake sit for an hour to cool and then refrigerate for 5 hours.

9. After the refrigeration is done, open the spring form pan and slice the cake.

Nutrition facts Nutrition facts per serving:

Calories 513; Fat 48g; Sodium 56mg; Carbs 21g; Protein 14g

BEAUTIFUL VANILLA PUDDING WITH BERRIES

So, right here at the end of this book lays an amazing surprise...STRAWBERRIES and BLUEBERRIES!!

Preparation Time: 15 minutes | Cooking Time: 18 minutes + 6h for refrigeration | Servings: 4

Ingredients:

1 cup Heavy Cream	1 tsp Vanilla
4 Egg Yolks	½ cup Sugar
4 tbsp Water + 1 ½ cups Water	4 Raspberries
½ cup Milk	4 Blueberries

Directions:

1. Turn on your cooker and select Sear/Sauté mode on Medium. Add four tablespoons for water and the sugar. Stir it constantly until it dissolves. Press Stop. Add milk, heavy cream, and vanilla. Stir it with a whisk until evenly combined.
2. Crack the eggs into a bowl and add a tablespoon of the cream mixture. Whisk it and then very slowly add the remaining cream mixture while whisking.
3. Fit the reversible rack at the bottom of the pot, and pour one and a half cup of water in it. Pour the mixture into four ramekins and place them on the rack.
4. Close the lid of the pot, secure the pressure valve, and select Pressure mode on High Pressure for 4 minutes. Press Start/Stop.
5. Once the timer has gone off, do a quick pressure release, and open the lid.
6. With a napkin in hand, carefully remove the ramekins onto a flat surface. Let them cool for about 15 minutes and then refrigerate them for 6 hours.
7. After 6 hours, remove them from the refrigerator and garnish them with the raspberries and blueberries.

Nutrition facts Nutrition facts per serving:

Calories 183; Fat 12.9g; Sodium 350mg; Carbs 12g; Protein 4g

LEMON-RICOTTA CHEESECAKE WITH STRAWBERRY

Pamper yourself with this zingy creamy nourishment. I love cheese a lot, so this cake is what I could splurge on morning, noon, and night. After so much of it, you are rest assured to be in a healthy state as it digests quickly with little to no fattening properties to worry about.

Preparation Time: 10 minutes | Cooking Time: 25 minutes | Servings: 6

Ingredients:

10 oz Cream Cheese

¼ cup Sugar

½ cup Ricotta Cheese

One Lemon, zested and juiced

2 Eggs, cracked into a bowl

1 tsp Lemon Extract

3 tbsp Sour Cream

1 ½ cups Water

10 Strawberries, halved to decorate

Directions:

1. In the electric mixer, add the cream cheese, quarter cup of sugar, ricotta cheese, lemon zest, lemon juice, and lemon extract. Turn on the mixer and mix the ingredients until a smooth consistency is formed. Adjust the sweet taste to liking with more sugar.

2. Reduce the speed of the mixer and add the eggs. Fold it in at low speed until it is fully incorporated. Make sure not to fold the eggs in high speed to prevent a cracker crust. Grease the spring form pan with cooking spray and use a spatula to spoon the mixture into the pan. Level the top with the spatula and cover it with foil.

3. Open the cooker, fit in the reversible rack, and pour in the water. Place the cake pan on the rack. Close the lid, secure the pressure valve, and select Pressure mode on High pressure for 15 minutes. Press Start/Stop.

4. Meanwhile, mix the sour cream and one tablespoon of sugar. Set aside.

5. Once the timer has gone off, do a natural pressure release for 10 minutes, then a quick pressure release to let out any extra steam, and open the lid.

6. Remove the rack with pan, place the spring form pan on a flat surface, and open it. Use a spatula to spread the sour cream mixture on the warm cake. Refrigerate the cake for 8 hours. Top with strawberries; slice it into 6 pieces and serve while firming.

Nutrition facts Nutrition facts per serving:

Calories 241; Fat 20g; Sodium 156mg; Carbs 8g; Protein 9g

CPSIA information can be obtained
at www.ICGtesting.com
Printed in the USA
BVHW010215250319
543594BV00010B/201/P